MY STYLISH
FRENCH
GIRLFRIENDS

MY STYLISH
FRENCH
GIRLFRIENDS

SHARON SANTONI

Creator of *My French Country Home*

PHOTOGRAPHS BY FRANCK SCHMITT

GIBBS SMITH
TO ENRICH AND INSPIRE HUMANKIND

For my family, with love.

—SHARON SANTONI

First Edition
19 18 17 16 15   5 4 3 2

Text © 2015 by Sharon Santoni
Photographs © 2015 by Franck Schmitt

Published by
Gibbs Smith
P.O. Box 667
Layton, Utah 84041

1.800.835.4993 orders
www.gibbs-smith.com

Designed by Sheryl Dickert
Page production by Renee Bond
Printed and bound in Hong Kong

Gibbs Smith books are printed on either recycled, 100% post-consumer waste, FSC-certified papers or on paper produced from sustainable PEFC-certified forest/controlled wood source. Learn more at www.pefc.org.

Library of Congress Cataloging-in-Publication Data

Santoni, Sharon.
 My stylish French girlfriends / Sharon Santoni ; Photographs by Franck Schmitt. — First Edition.
      pages cm
 ISBN 978-1-4236-3787-5
 1. Interior decoration—France. 2. Women—Homes and haunts—France. 3. Women—France—Social life and customs—21st century. 4. Santoni, Sharon—Friends and associates. I. Title.
 NK2049.A1S26 2015
 747.082'0944—dc23
                                        2015002110

CONTENTS

INTRODUCTION

Having lived in France for longer than I lived in my native England, I feel totally at home here. But while I may be fully settled, married to a Frenchman and with four Anglo-French children, I can still see France and the French from the outside. I enjoy taking a few steps back to appreciate the essential "Frenchness" of a beautiful building; of a long delicious meal; the charm of a farmers market or indeed the stylishness of my French girlfriends.

It is this insider's view, this private, discreet side to French living and to the French women I know that I wish to portray. Women who work every day, with passion, who love to take care of their homes, their families, themselves.

As I approached women I know — some who live in grand chateaux, others in charming little country cottages, or Parisian apartments — asking them to be part of the book, I was amazed and touched at the reception I received. Each girlfriend was immediately enthusiastic. And although none of them are particularly used to being photographed, they were all highly professional in the way they welcomed us for the photos shoots and interviews.

These portraits of women and homes show a side of France that visitors don't normally get to see. I deliberately sought out women from all over the country, reaching from Calais in the north to Provence in the south. Each girlfriend was chosen because she has a story to tell and a great lifestyle to portray. I picked friends of all ages, because it is through living our lives that our characters grow; some faces may have a few more lines, but that is only because they have smiled more. And with age comes a new self-confidence, a self-assuredness.

We often hear about how inspirational the French woman is — stylish, confident, *'bien dans sa peau,"* (comfortable in her own skin). And this was certainly the case among the women in this book. For our photo shoots, none of the girlfriends asked for any special lighting or makeup; the beauty and character that you see here is how they really are.

There is an overriding creative theme amongst my girlfriends because I am fortunate to know many people who create on a daily basis. They paint, cook, sculpt, make couture gowns, restore breathtaking buildings, style stunning homes, and express themselves in many other ways.

Not surprisingly, considering that they are all women I know, some of the girls were already friends with each other. Fred rides with Cornélie; Alicia is a neighbor to Cécile; Nathalie and Sabine are sisters-in-law; Celestina and Clarisse are close friends and also work together.

There were also some amusing coincidences during the making of the book, like the delivery of Evelyne's champagne to Claire's chateau while we were taking our photos there. Nothing to do with us; the champagne was from an admiring art collector.

Or the surprise when we learned that Valérie's future daughter-in-law would be wearing a dress by Celestina for her wedding, or that one of Ysabel's paintings was already hanging in Evelyne's home.

All of this made for some lively conversation when nearly all the girlfriends got together for a group photo at the iconic Merci store in Paris. Merci welcomed us with open arms, proclaiming that they love strong women with great projects, and we had fun taking the photos at the entrance to the store and over a long lunch afterwards in their library restaurant.

With talented photographer Franck Schmitt, it took us six months to complete the photos for the book. We flew and drove all over France, staying in chateaux, beach houses, or wherever the girlfriends called home; we were made to feel welcome. Apart from fresh flowers, there was no staging or styling done for our pictures; the photos simply portray the way they live each day. They let us take photos in their homes, at their work, while they entertained and during their leisure time. Their generosity was boundless.

From a candlelit dinners with lobster and champagne, to a barbecue eaten beside a river, to picnics enjoyed on their property or on a mountainside, each girlfriend went out of her way to make us feel welcome.

From the moment I started working on the book, I don't think a day passed when I didn't pronounce the word "privilege," for that, above all, is what making this book has truly been: the privilege of introducing you to my stylish French girlfriends.

ALICIA

The antique fair at Chatou, on the outskirts of Paris, is absolutely one of my favorites. It is a concentration of the best French dealers all in one place for ten days at a time, an ideal place for meeting new antique dealers who come from all over France to show at the fair.

Discovering new sources is always fun: sometimes it's a dealer from Brittany who specializes in paintings; other times it'll be someone from the south who sells century-old dinner services and flatware. Even if you don't buy at each stand, the dealers are always glad to chat about their work. That's how I first met Alicia.

My aunt had asked me to source an old French farm table for her kitchen. I promised to keep my eyes open and set off the next day for Chatou, her table added to my own wish list.

As I walked through the fair, buying here and there, Alicia's stand caught my eye. It was beautifully staged, with a country feel to it, exactly the style I love. She had painted wooden furniture with real patina, some wonderful textiles, a few small paintings and a farm table that looked perfect for my aunt!

I introduced myself and chatted with Alicia. She was younger than me, but I quickly realized how knowledgeable she was. It was clear that each item she sold was important to her, and that she traveled all over France to find her treasures. Her bright blue eyes divulged the passion she feels for her work. Before I knew it, we had chatted for an hour and arranged to meet at her warehouse the following week.

For her, selling antiques is not about decoration, but about the beauty of an object and how it can fit into a home. — *"Il faut que l'objet trouve sa place."* She takes a poetic approach to her work:

happy when she finds the right home for an object, happy when the new owner understands the beauty.

Alicia chooses not to have a store, as she is unwilling to be tied down to boutique hours. Instead she shows at fairs and occasionally receives clients in her warehouse on a neighboring farm. The first time I visited her storage, I took a friend with me. We drove into the farm courtyard and through a huge barn door, past tractors and combine harvesters, until at the far end of the barn, Alicia's display opened up before us, all the more beautiful because of its unlikely setting.

Alicia's eloquence belies a rocky educational path. As a child she was unhappy at school, ill at ease with the formality of the French school system. She wanted to tread her own path, to discover her own truths. At the age of fifteen she left school and joined a circus. She did stunt horseback riding; she handled falcons, charmed snakes and juggled. Not the typical route for a young girl from a fine family. At the time it certainly can't have been easy to quit the system and go against conventional truth, and her family found it difficult to watch her struggle, but time has proven her right. Away from the discipline and regulations of traditional education, Alicia has invented her own life. She is an autodidact, widely read, and a lover of music and art.

As well as understanding the antiques she sells, Alicia is also a gifted stylist. Today she is in demand for staging weddings and events in the green countryside of the Perche, to the west of Paris. She packs up her truck with furniture and accessories, and arrives with huge bouquets of freshly cut meadow flowers to complete her signature style.

9

Alicia's stand at the brocante fair: garden seed packets, antique demijohns and wine glasses; set off with simple blue cornflowers; odds and ends for garden or indoors; a journal displayed with scattered wooden letters.

A delightful mix of antiques and meadow flowers inviting clients to take their time to browse.

iscipline in every area of her life, Alicia lives in a manner that is as eco-friendly as possible, and her work as a *brocanteuse* fits into that ethic. As she says, "Why buy something new when there is so much beautiful furniture already existing?"

For Alicia, everyday beauty is vital. In her kitchen all her dry goods are stored in tall green glass jars. The jars are antique, of course, and the perfect example of combining the practical with the aesthetic. Her plates are works of art created by her husband Matthias.

The mother-son bond between Alicia and her son Jules is very strong, and to compensate for being away from home for the fairs, she is sure to create some quality time with Jules whenever she is at home, be it a picnic in the forest with their dog, or a fishing party by the river. Their simple lifestyle is fun. They have a big circle of friends and Jules will have wonderful memories of his childhood days.

Alicia lives by her convictions. She has a natural beauty that transcends passing fashion, and like the young girl who first ran away to the circus, she is never afraid to tread her individual path.

An infusion of homegrown verbena, served in her husband's hand-cast bowls.

The simple kitchen is bathed in light from the window open on to the garden.

The garden provides a peaceful setting for the old stone cottage, and in the summer months windows and doors are always wide open.

A vintage trailer forms a cute summerhouse in a corner of the garden.

Being on the road so often, Alicia is sure to make time for special moments with her son, Jules—a picnic and a country walk with the ever-faithful Simba at their side.

CATHERINE

s a little girl, Catherine dreamed of living in a chateau and preparing delicious meals for long tables of friends and family. A chateau sat above the town where she grew up and she fantasized about life inside its walls. Her upbringing, though, was much simpler.

Catherine remembers her father starting work at dawn every day selling seafood fresh from the fishermen's boats; her grandfather spent his life selling the finest cured hams and meats in the region. Like these men before her, she was drawn to the role of provider, of being the one who nurtures and feeds. True to the tradition of warm hospitality in the north of France, Catherine loves to *faire chapelle,* a regional expression that means "to open your house to family and friends."

Catherine's family includes her husband and childhood sweetheart, Guy, and their three tall, handsome sons. Catherine and Guy are a close-knit couple. They were both born and raised in the north of France, a region where the climate can be grey but where the local character is renowned for its generosity and kindness. Their sons practice Guy's mantra of "work hard and play hard" and have followed his footsteps down to the moody grey seashore, where they are all passionate kite surfers.

Catherine and Guy both believe in making dreams come true. As Guy puts it, "We only have one life; there is no point if we don't enjoy it!" When Guy had an opportunity to sell his company and start afresh, the family was torn between two ideas. He wanted to buy a small house and a large sailboat and spend six months of the year on the sea, while Catherine still dreamed of her chateau and longed to create a bed-and-breakfast.

Guy acknowledged that he already had a career he loved in the world of surfing and decided it was Catherine's turn to fulfill her dream. Together they set off to find a chateau for sale.

They wanted to stay in the region and first visited the Chateau de la Marine, but it was beyond their budget. At one point this chateau belonged to the French Navy, from where it got its name. It had a beautiful view over the sea, and Catherine and Guy both loved it, but they stuck to their figures and regretfully continued looking.

Months of fruitless searching ensued until, disheartened, they went off sailing for three months. When they came back home, they heard that the Chateau de la Marine remained unsold and decided to make an offer. It was meant to be: their offer was accepted and Catherine's dream suddenly became a reality.

21

The ocean is never far away. And it's a pleasure to shop for fresh seafood and stroll along the beach before returning home to cook for the family.

Remodeling the chateau was a team effort. Catherine and Guy embraced the renovation project with energy and enthusiasm. The chateau was built in 1870 and rebuilt following a fire in 1900. They wanted to respect the history of the property while creating a place that would be elegant and welcoming, where they would be proud to welcome guests and friends.

Once the major work was completed, Catherine started the interior design. Inspired by the hotels she loved, she created a clear picture of her own chateau's style. The color palette would be elegantly muted, the furniture comfortable, the bathrooms divine. She wanted her guests to feel that they were visiting with friends in the country.

Catherine bought carefully, choosing suppliers for their quality and style. She loves to hunt through antique and brocante stores, and in her part of France the choice is particularly rich. She often came home with silverware or a pair of bedside tables in the trunk of her car, small touches to make her chateau even more inviting and unique.

When Catherine wasn't decorating she was planning. Part of the great plan was that she would cook wonderful meals for their guests. Her beautiful, luminous kitchen had direct access to the family dining room in the old chapel. Here her cooking and preparation is centered around her pride and joy, a La Cornue stove, which is French cuisine royalty.

Catherine has always enjoyed cooking for her own family and for friends, but a birthday gift took her one step further towards fine gourmet cuisine: lessons at the Parisian school of the famous French chef Alain Ducasse.

For several months she jumped on a train to Paris each week and spent a day learning new techniques. One week it was pastry, the next chocolate, then meat or fish. Here Catherine learned the secrets of the professional chefs and gained the confidence she needed to prepare meals for her future clients.

Good meals start with excellent ingredients, and for the chateau's cuisine she does what she has always done for her family: shop for fresh food every day. She buys at the local markets and serves only seasonal produce. Being by the sea, Catherine has made a specialty of preparing seafood such as lobster, crab and shellfish.

Her reputation quickly grew locally and she decided to open her restaurant to guests beyond her B&B clients. Numbers will always be limited to maintain her high standards, but her name is one of those confidential addresses that her guests like to share with those they love best.

These days the table that Catherine dreamt of as a little girl really is long and full, and the chateau that seemed so unattainable is hers to share.

The spacious family dining room with a view out to sea.

Attention to detail and a beautiful table are as important
as the food that is served.

When restoring the chateau, Catherine and Guy were careful to preserve architectural details, which adds to the soul of their home.

The sitting room, where guests can enjoy a coffee and plan out their day.

The muted tones of Catherine's décor feel luxurious and welcoming.

Each elegant guest room has a balcony with a view over the garden.

Details from the bedroom suites, where Catherine's special touches make guests comfortable.

CÉCILE

discovered Cécile quite by chance. While out driving one afternoon, a sign for a boutique and tea room posted on a tiny lane in the middle of nowhere had my foot flat on the brake. The entrance was pretty and inviting and I was ready for a cup of tea, so I decided to explore.

One step inside the little store and I was under its charms. Cécile welcomed me warmly, we chatted, and within ten minutes of meeting her I asked if I could write about her. Some friendships are just meant to be.

We have a lot in common. We are both first and foremost family animals. We dote on our children, our husbands are great, and we both put family life ahead of other demands.

Since that first day, I have also discovered that Cécile is a rock. She is the girl to turn to in an emergency, the pragmatic, clear thinker with a quick sense of humor who can help you see the light through the darkest tunnel and appreciate the funny side to any crisis.

In the '90s Cécile and her husband Franck decided to leave the rush and bustle of Paris and raise their three boys in the countryside of le Perche. This is a beautiful region of stone-built villages, tall church spires, green fields and rolling hills.

Franck was nostalgic for the simple country life that he had tasted with his grandparents, and Cécile knew that she could be more creative starting her own business in the country than continuing in the demanding job she held in Paris.

But while it's easy to say "We'll move to the country," working out the details can be challenging.

Franck was already a busy freelance journalist, author and photographer, so their move didn't change his work, but Cécile needed to find an activity that would integrate them as a family into the local scene, and yet leave her the time and space to be creative and to build the home they yearned for. Bright, dynamic and sociable, Cécile got involved in the local tourist office and quickly led the team. The work was a great way to discover her new home region, but it didn't give her the creative outlet that she craved.

Everything changed when Cécile and Franck had the opportunity of buying a larger property with space not only for the family to live but also for Cécile to create. Once their new property was purchased, their country life really began to take shape.

In Cécile's hands, the very simple old stone house became a warm and welcoming home. Bright colors dominate the bedrooms and living space, and the house is furnished with an eclectic mix of brocante finds and designer pieces. Her sense of humor is apparent in all corners of her home. From the guest cottage in the garden that is dubbed "the chicken coop," to her brightly colored décor, to the way she deals with problems along the way with a smile rather than a frown, Cécile's happy attitude brings levity to her everyday life in the country.

33

It's the tiny details around the house that show Cécile's sense of humor, even the birdcage is given a funny twist with a butcher's price tag on the top.

An eclectic display of goods in the store in the old barn says it all.

Fifties, the Jack Russell, enjoys her time in the family room, where vibrant color occasionally punctuates the chic black, grey and white color scheme.

All over the house, Cécile finds ways to display her favorite brocante finds, like these old clock faces, whose pops of color brighten the hallway.

Her tearoom is warm and welcoming, with the store name spelled out in vintage letters on the wall.

Be it in the "chicken coop" guest cottage or in her own bedroom, Cécile is never afraid of using bright colors.

The garden shed in a corner of the potager is enhanced with antique watering cans and decorative pigeons on the roof.

Flanked by flowering cherry trees, the guest cottage is pretty in any season.

Chickens, ducks and geese are allowed to roam the garden.

One of the beauties of buying old property in France is the number of buildings that come with the main house. Here was no exception, and Cécile knew that the old stone barn with the high ceiling would make a great display area. Then she thought, why not turn it into a store?

Why not a store? Well, there are plenty of reasons, but the main one was that their tiny village is no more than a handful of houses and even the nearest town is small and sleepy. Cécile reacted in her usual optimistic manner: "*C'est pas grave* . . . it doesn't matter! If I offer something good enough then people will come!"

She was right. Her first year of business was a success and she grew more confident, opening every weekend for teas and brunches, selling from the store and welcoming guests to her little weekend cottage. She used social networks and word of mouth to publicize the store.

Four years later she has expanded, and her country address draws clients from afar: Parisians with weekend homes in the area, antique buffs searching for new brocante pieces, and people living locally for whom Cécile has become a byword for tea and chocolate cakes and a wonderful address for home décor.

Finding goods for the store is a full-time job. Cécile loves to hunt through local brocante fairs for new pieces. A table that needs fixing or a piece of furniture requiring a new coat of paint finds a new lease on life in her hands. Wherever she travels she deliberately seeks out local craftsmen in the hope of finding new suppliers to bring an exotic and designer flavor to her country shop.

Today Cécile is a good friend and the road from my house to hers is well worn. Whenever I send new clients over to her store, they always come back amazed by the creative and interesting life that Cécile and Franck have made for themselves in the middle of nowhere.

CELESTINA

Celestina works all day surrounded by women: the seamstresses in her ateliers, her assistants in her offices and, of course, those who come to lay claim to one of her creations. Because Celestina creates unique and beautiful bridal gowns, and the mere mention of her name is enough to make future brides swoon. Her clients come to her to fulfill dreams; they trust her to interpret their wishes, and, like a satin ribbon around a lace waistband, she is woven into the most important day of their lives — their wedding day.

Watching a wedding dress fitting in Celestina's atelier is like a scene on the stage of some magical, dream-like theater. In her chic, silver-grey salon, Celestina receives her clients at all stages of the dressmaking. She meets hundreds of women each week. The young bride-to-be rarely arrives alone, and Celestina meets her mother, her sisters, her grandmother, and her bridesmaids. It makes for a lot of ladies together, all keen to give their opinions, all keen to see this dress as the most beautiful dress ever made and the most important element of the impending big day.

Celestina carries the show. With her bubbling, generous personality, she talks all the time: "Ah, that is so beautiful"; "You look divine, *c'est magnifique*"; "That is exactly the dress for you." She moves around the young woman, pinning lace, adding a pleat, taking in a little at the waist, inserting pins as visual instructions for her seamstresses once the dress returns to the couture room.

Each bride emerges from her fitting with her head high, a smile on her lips, confident that Celestina has understood her wishes and will be able to make her the dress she dreams of.

This is a privileged address in Paris, and Celestina is fiercely proud of her atelier and the gifted women who work there. It is a luxurious haven of peace, a sea of greys and whites, and of pearls, lace and netting that are worthy of any of the city's greatest couture houses.

Celestina is the turbo engine of her design house. She is the one who sketches the designs, who meets each bride and interprets each dress. Today her name is known across the world because her energy has taken her there. She insists that she could never have done this alone but relies on the team that has been with her for twenty-one years.

The chic reception area of Celestina's couture salon, where brides-to-be get their first glimpse of the atelier.

The initial stage for each dress is drawing the pattern. Then a talented seamstress in the atelier follows Celestina's instructions meticulously to bring the dress to life.

Celestina sketches every bridal gown. This is where true haute couture begins.

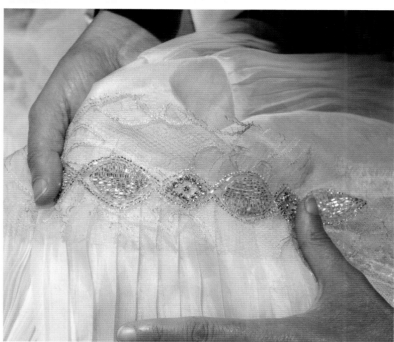

In the display window that opens on to the quiet little street, passersby can imagine the beauty that is created behind these walls.

One of Celestina's stunning creations, caught in the salon spotlights.

Celestina's success has not come overnight. She grew up in the north of France with her parents, a modest hardworking couple. Her father was a miner and her mother a seamstress. Never could they have dreamt that one day their daughter would have her own couture house in Paris and would sell her creations on both sides of the Atlantic Ocean.

Celestina was ambitious and as soon as she was old enough she came to Paris. In order to pay for her studies she combined working for a publisher with furthering her own education. She was successful in her work at the publishers, and en route to a good career. She could have stayed in the job and progressed, but at the age of thirty, she decided that she needed to be more creative. Something of her mother's talent as a seamstress guided her to start work in a Parisian couture house, where for three years she learned all there was to know about cutting a pattern and fitting a dress.

By the time she finished her apprenticeship, she knew she wanted her own couture name. She immediately thought of designing wedding dresses, of working exclusively in white, and quite soon she had her first employees; the very first members of her team are still with her today.

Celestina's story is truly a rags-to-riches fairy tale and she is grateful to everyone who has helped her along the path. It's probably this recognition of needing help to succeed in life that makes her so keen to support the children around her.

Her own daughter, Rose, loves the theater and has her mother's total backing, and Celestina is also godmother to nine children. They meet for lunch, she is involved in their education, and most of all, she hopes to inspire them by her example of working hard and progressing step by step.

If you ask Celestina what she still dreams about, she answers, "To remarry and be happy with the love of my life." At least she'll be sure of wearing the perfect wedding dress!

CHARLOTTE

The first time I met Charlotte was at a little *brocante* fair in a village in Normandy. She had brought along a few items to sell, and I was immediately intrigued by this beautiful lady with such an array of carefully curated treasures.

I remember picking up a cake stand from her display. "*Oui, c'est très joli*; it's very pretty," she said. "It has a small crack right here, you see?" She pointed to the hairline crack on the blue-and-white china. "But that just makes it more charming; that way it has a story to tell, *non?*"

We chatted for a while and I liked her discreet manner. She was slightly reserved and yet had a warm smile. She was the sort of person whose confidence you had to gain first, and then hope that maybe friendship would come later. Today I count her as a friend whose company I enjoy and whose talent I admire. If we find ourselves at the same fair, we always take time to share a coffee and compare our loot: a monogrammed sheet, a beautiful white pitcher, or maybe a small painting.

Along with her husband, Alain, Charlotte divides her time between Paris and Normandy, loving the peace and openness of the countryside, but also enjoying a weekly trip back into Paris for a day or two, just to keep in touch with the capital, to stay in tune with what makes the city hum.

Charlotte grew up in the Normandy countryside, in an era when generations spent time together and families were the mainstay of everyday life. She learned to read with her grandfather, but not the way one might expect one would learn to read, by sitting at a table with pretty picture books and large, clear letters spelling out the alphabet. Charlotte's reading apprenticeship took place in the botanical gardens of the local town. There she learned to read the zinc plant labels stuck into the ground at the foot of each bush and tree, carefully deciphering the scrawled writing that spelled out the names in Latin.

She read the labels aloud, without understanding, simply happy to please her grandfather while caught up in the mystery and poetry of those words, which held magical meanings behind their syllables.

That today she collects so much zinc is surely a throwback to those early years, reading from the plant tags and spending time in her grandparents' gardens and *potagers*, where the metal was used for the everyday tools and appendages that we now find so rustically charming.

Her grandmothers, too, helped fashion her taste for the beautiful. Both women were fine seamstresses and Charlotte spent hours sitting with them, sorting threads and buttons, playing with scraps of lace, and watching their needles make their tiny, perfect stitches.

Her teenage years took her to Paris. At that time, beyond the center of the city to the north was a town called St. Ouen, where people sold old objects, long before the notion of "vintage" existed. The flea market then was a collection of small antique shops and restoration ateliers, with a vibrant creative streak hidden just beneath the surface.

To her parents' great consternation, Charlotte spent many hours at St. Ouen, discovering this new world full of artists, where each object had a story to tell and a beauty to reveal. This is where she met Alain, a tall, handsome artist who later became her husband.

Curating and displaying favorite pieces becomes an art form in Charlotte's home. Everything has its place; every piece holds a story.

A sideboard becomes a unique display area with a delightful mix of lights and glass.

The house may be carefully styled, but that doesn't stop it from being easy-going and welcoming.

Charlotte's first real job was as a sales girl for Christian Dior on Avenue Montaigne. There, she discovered another atmosphere, with different codes and languages. In the shop, attention to detail was vital and perfection was non-negotiable. The little girl who had found so much pleasure in her grandmothers' sewing rooms was now at the heart of luxury French couture, with all of its rites and traditions.

The contrast between her leisure time in the flea market and her working day *chez* Monsieur Dior was food to her soul — and to her innate curiosity. She fed on the beauty of the lavish fabrics and designs and was fascinated by the exclusive couture clientele. In this refined atmosphere her eye was trained to appreciate the luxury of fine workmanship.

Charlotte does not like to be called a collector, but rather a curator. She continues to hunt at fairs, but not with the thirst of a vendor needing new items to sell. She goes to fairs in the hope of being surprised, in the hope of having an encounter with the unexpected, of seeing the unlikely with her eyes wide open, as they have always been, taking in the world around her, and enjoying every new experience along the way.

When you meet Charlotte, you sense immediately that she has a rare gift as a curator and a stylist, with her sure eye for associating objects, colors and textures. The arrangements of objects around her home and garden look effortless and natural, but it is an art that she has refined throughout her life. The same goes for her wardrobe. Whether she is in the country or in Paris, her dress sense is impeccably stylish: she is one of those women who other women want to resemble.

Charlotte and Alain can take the time to indulge their own needs and interests. Alain still loves to paint, and twice a year, in the garden of their country home, they invite friends and family to an outdoor picnic — an occasion for Alain to open up his atelier and for Charlotte to do what she does best — enchant.

When her guests arrive, they park their cars on the country lane outside her home and walk down a path to the blue garden gate set into the wall. Once inside, they find the barn and garden presented as a showroom for Alain and Charlotte's creations. The lawn is scattered with small tables and chairs; friends come with their picnics and rugs and the day is spent enjoying good conversation and the simple pleasure of sharing.

Charlotte and Alain are at that comfortable stage in their lives when they can sit back and enjoy, while taking the time to savor, to create, and to share that pleasure with those they hold dear.

CHRISTELLE

The first time I met Christelle was at a fair in the middle of a field in Normandy, at 6 o'clock on a misty Sunday morning. I didn't expect to find her at that fair, though I had seen an article about her in a local magazine in which she talked about her life in Normandy and her passion for brocante and antiques. As I read the piece attentively, I was intrigued by this pretty young woman with such a sure eye and faultless taste. In the magazine photo, she wore a big grey and white scarf around her neck.

As I walked through the field that morning, I was drawn toward an interesting display. I noticed the young woman behind the beautifully laid out goods and recognized her immediately, especially when I spotted the grey scarf lying with her coat on a chair.

We chatted, I bought a couple of bits from her, and since then I have become a regular visitor to her charming country store nestled inside the home she shares with her husband and two children. Each time I walk into her home and store, I am always thrilled by a new display, rearranged furniture or her latest brocante find.

Christelle has bought and collected all her life, learning the trade from her mother, grandmother and aunt. When she was little and already living in Normandy, she used to walk home from school and stop off at her aunt's brocante store, where she loved to sort glassware or arrange china. Christelle has clear memories of those days, in particular of the workshop where the furniture was restored, polished and brought back to life.

When she moved with her husband into their home on a fairly tight budget, she quickly came up with ways to make everything stylish. With the arrival of each child came the extension of the house to make space for everyone to be comfortable.

Christelle loved to hunt for brocante, first for her own home, and then to sell to clients who admired her style. Before long, the photos on her blog caught the attention of overseas buyers; potential clients visiting Paris started making the journey out to Normandy to visit her store during its weekends-only open hours. Her clients always smile as they walk through the garden gate and see her house and gardens spread before them — Christelle loves the ambiance that a home-based store can create. Clients feel so comfortable that they stay a while, and a shopping spree feels more like visiting with friends.

There is a seasonal aspect to Christelle's work. The traditional country brocante fairs, where she finds so many of her treasures, do not run during the winter months, so there is no need to get out of bed at unearthly hours on a Sunday or to drive for miles down country lanes at that time of year. Consequently, the winter is when Christelle sews and creates. The ideas that have been forming in her mind through the summer find the space and time to come to life in her atelier, where she can be found busy at work behind her sewing machine.

65

LOGEMENT
A LOUER

Her store is well stocked but never too busy. On display are rolls of home-spun linen and old clock faces; Christelle gives her clients ideas for styling in their own homes.

Shutters, painted drawers, wooden filing boxes – Christelle's style is a mix of industrial and patina; each object finds a new purpose and a fresh beauty.

Christelle's house is often used for photo shoots and displayed in magazines and books. Of course the recognition is nice, but she is also aware that the cameras are invading her private family home. Christelle cautiously stages her house for these shoots so that her family's real life is not on public display. Once the pictures are taken and the cameras have gone, Christelle methodically returns her family's more personal possessions to their rightful places. Though there is some compromise with privacy, Christelle would never want to have a store in town because it would take her away from home too much and she would lose the luxury of working on her own ground.

But with this practical arrangement comes a balancing act that is the dilemma of any young working woman — combining her own business with family life. She is entirely supported in her endeavors by her husband, David, and she will always put her two sons, Paul and Mathieu, before her work, but the line can be fine and difficult to walk. One of her favorite ways to show her love for

her boys and to spend time alone with her family is cooking. Her newly renovated kitchen is bathed in beautiful natural light and is a room where the family comes together.

While Christelle is cooking, the boys get on with school homework on the long farm table. She loves to improvise her meals rather than follow a recipe. The women in her family have always cooked well and she knows the importance of cooking simply with fresh ingredients. Meals are delicious and well balanced, and friends are always pleased to be invited to her table. She has quite a reputation for her meringues, which, I can attest, are simply perfect.

So it is as her boys hit their teenage years, Christelle continues to fulfill her role as mother and wife, caring for the men in her life and also satisfying her need to create in her store and atelier. Finding the right balance for a harmonious and fulfilled life in the country is not always easy. Christelle has found her own very special way to achieve it.

The new kitchen is light and airy; the style is country brocante with a touch of industrial.

On one side of the kitchen is the dining table with its mismatched chairs; vintage letters for the name of each family member are displayed on the wall.

Furniture moves around often in the home, here an old set of industrial drawers is used as storage space in the office.

Christelle has great talent for combining elements and textures without ever making her rooms look cluttered. Simple paper lampshades are draped with tiny lights rather than lit from inside.

The small garden is pretty and well tended. Visitors to the store walk past the main house and have time to admire the roses and garden vignettes before reaching the door.

CLAIRE

laire doesn't need a lot of sleep and it is just as well. Besides painting fabulous canvases for clients all around the world and restoring and painting the interior of her 14th-century chateau, she also somehow finds the time to create and maintain a stunning *potager* in the large square courtyard at the heart of her property.

Claire is the most prolific artist I know. Her canvases are full of billowing, dreamy flowers across misty landscapes, or monochrome forests, or individual blooms that float above shining backgrounds of silver or gold leaf. Her solid botanical knowledge allows her to portray individual flowers in great detail. Claire trained in fine art in Paris and at the age of eighteen sold a painting to a friend's sister. It was the first sale of many to come.

During her long career she has partnered with galleries, but today she prefers to work alone, organizing her own shows and painting to order for private clients.

I have been fortunate enough to see her paintings on display at her home and it is even more impressive than seeing them in a gallery, as their delicate detail is thrown into contrast against the stark backdrop of her austere stone chateau.

It wasn't her intention to purchase an enormous chateau. She and her husband, Pierre, wanted to leave Paris and were looking for a small property. Claire had been working hard and found the continual painting and exhibitions very tiring. She was ready to settle into a smaller space and create in a more confidential manner.

Claire and Pierre were drawn to the center of France, with its remote villages and independence from Paris. Their aim was to downsize, but when they saw a small ad for a 14th-century chateau, curiosity got the better of them and they arranged a visit. They met up with the realtor outside the chateau, halfway up a mountain. Four hours after walking under the arched stone entrance, having toured all the buildings and explored the dungeon and the acres of forest and field, they turned to the estate agent and announced their intention to buy!

He laughed in disbelief. The chateau was vast, the roofs were caving in, and there was no electricity, no heating, and only one water tap for the whole building — and it had stood abandoned for forty years.

This didn't put them off. Claire is a great one for using her positive energy to make things happen. Pierre is practical minded and can turn his hands to almost anything. His background is very diverse: he's been everything from a teacher, to a pilot, to a boat builder. He is imperturbable, and today, besides continuing the restoration of the chateau and the day-to-day organization, he also handles all of Claire's PR and the shipping of her paintings.

Their first winter in the chateau was spent with only one fire lit and no bathtub. New friends in the village allowed them to use their shower whenever they wanted. At the chateau, windows needed repairing, walls were damp from the missing roof tiles, and indoors the temperature way below freezing unless they stood close to the roaring fire, in which case they gained a balmy two degrees.

77

The wood for the log fire in the salon is stacked in industrial style metal racks against a wide wall panel completely painted by Claire.

A finished canvas in the studio waits beside a vase of fresh peonies; flowers are ever-present inspiration and ambiance.

The ample kitchen is simply furnished. It is a favorite spot for the dogs when they are not with Claire in her studio.

Claire has painted the walls in the long dining room and the many bedrooms; the wall art warms the large spaces. Each room has its own theme and particular flowers, but the overall style flows smoothly throughout.

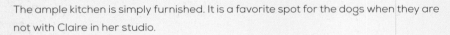

A wide stone staircase leads up to the main entrance to the chateau. On either side of the stairs stands an imposing stone pillar, which Claire surrounds with bushes of box and perennials in old zinc tubs.

It is from the potager, set into the garden in the center of the chateau, that the size of the property is clearest. The main wings look out over the view that stretches for miles below.

They tamed the building, advancing step by step, methodically dealing with each problem as it came rather than getting lost in the immensity of the project. The chateau was constructed over several hundred years, between the 13th and 18th centuries. In the 19th century many of the original details were destroyed in the name of modernization, but the magnificent bones were there for Claire and Pierre to reveal and enhance during their two-year renovation. Their hard work has paid off, and today they have a beautiful enfilade of large rooms with high ceilings and wooden parquet floors, with more guest rooms on another floor.

To celebrate the end of the major work and to thank all the local people who had helped them so much, they held an open exhibition of Claire's work, staged in all corners of the enormous property. Visitors were welcome to wander from the stables to the kitchen, to the studio and even through the bedrooms. There was as much interest in the renovation as the artwork.

Claire's atelier is in a wing at the rear of the chateau, in a long, tall orangery bathed in natural light. The far end of the glass-fronted room is where Pierre patiently applies the gold and silver leaf that serves as a base to some of her canvases. It is striking what complementary partners Claire and her husband are. Thanks to Pierre's support backstage, Claire has more time to paint, and more room to expand and grow.

Together they think outside the box and find innovative solutions to problems. When they tired of hauling logs up an outside staircase to feed the fireplace in their first-floor salon, Pierre found a conveyor belt from a gravel pit and snapped it up. He installed it between the huge log reserve and the window to the salon, and *voila!* Job done!

In the center of the orangery, Claire displays her most recent paintings. This is also where her dogs lie sleeping while they wait for her to finish work. Her studio space is at the entrance to the orangery. Here she always has a couple of canvases perched on huge easels. Her stool is positioned centrally, with a table for her palette and her pots of paint on one side, and a jungle of fresh flowers displayed together in a group of vases on the other side. These are not there by chance: they are reference material for her paintings, but also there because she cannot live without them.

Claire's life is full of flowers. Those she paints and those she grows and displays in every room of her house. And when flowers don't fit the bill, she brings huge branches of trees inside, slices of forest, towering above her as they stand balanced in tall, heavy glass vases. The branches arrive indoors in the early summer and the vases are topped up with water through the season, until the leaves gently turn color and fall to the floor.

When I last visited Claire, we spent the end of the afternoon in her *potager*, tending the plants and drinking in the fantastic view. I turned to her, curiosity getting the better of me, and asked, "What more could you possibly want, Claire? You have a loving husband who supports you in everything you do; you live in a beautiful chateau with a view to die for; you have a talent that most people can never even dream of. Surely this is it, you have reached the *summum* of your art?"

She smiled, looked dreamily out to the horizon, golden in the evening light, and quietly said, "There is still so much to discover in my work, I haven't managed yet to show exactly what I feel. I think I can do better."

CLARISSE

How could I talk about my girlfriends without including a girl who shares my passion for flowers?

Clarisse is tall and slim, with silver hair and a warm smile. Her natural elegance sets the tone in her Paris store, where I stopped one afternoon and found her listening attentively to a lady who wanted to gift a small bouquet to a neighbor.

The client was evidently a regular customer to the boutique, as she didn't try to tell Clarisse which sort of flowers she wanted to buy but rather told her about the friend she was buying for: "She has a very elegant apartment, her curtains are deep grey and she collects antique silverware. I am invited to dinner this evening; I would like to bring her a small bouquet for her table and maybe present it in this silver bowl. It is my birthday gift to her." The lady reached into a small canvas tote and drew out a charming antique sugar bowl standing on four tiny feet.

Clarisse smiled, asked how many people would be at the dinner, presumably for the table size, and without hesitation reached for some white anemones with deep grey centers, some branches of senecio, stems of privet with its black winter berries, a handful of purple black pansies and a few wisps of grey-green thyme. In a matter of minutes she had cropped the stems and created a perfect table centerpiece in the pretty bowl and wrapped it so her client could carry it safely to the dinner party that night.

Clarisse is more than a florist; she is a poet. Her rhymes take the shape of long stems and billowing branches and her words are buds and blooms.

Her passion grew early. As a child in Brittany she spent time with a friend of her parents, a female horticulturist who was happy to have a young girl hanging around, helping out in the potting shed, watering seedlings, taking cuttings, and learning to nurture and to understand the differences among the plants and flowers. It may not have been a formal training, but it allowed Clarisse to discover her vocation and reveal her artistic and horticultural talent.

In the atelier behind her Paris showroom, Clarisse and her exclusively female team work at a long wooden table, assembling bouquets, filling vases and dispatching their works of art to homes, offices and hotels around the city. Her window displays are well known in her *quartier* and some people make the detour each day just to see what's new. Passers by slow down, smile, reach for their phone or camera and share an image with the world. In her store there is an awareness of being part of the *quartier* but also part of Paris as a whole, because Clarisse is one of very few elite floral artists in the city.

Working as a florist demands dedication. Clarisse has to visit the wholesale flower market on the outskirts of the city before dawn to bring home the most beautiful blooms. She leaves her apartment before the city is awake, spends a couple of hours with her suppliers picking out her favorite blooms, and gets to her store in time for the start of the workday. Once she arrives it takes two hours to position all the new flowers in the showroom before she can turn her attention to filling orders.

Interruptions are frequent in the shop, especially from the suppliers that come to her door. White trucks stop outside the boutique, blocking traffic in the tiny street, but nobody seems to

87

Clarisse spends her days surrounded by flowers, from the wholesale market to her boutique, where bouquets are assembled with care.

mind. The truck doors open to reveal the homegrown foliage that Clarisse could never find at the market: raspberry stalks, cow parsley, and wild euphorbia — the sort of flower that makes her arrangements stand out.

Over the twenty years she has been running her own store, Clarisse has always felt a pressure to find the right balance between her work, which is her passion, and the demands of family life. Her days are long and demanding, but she loves her job. The shop stays open late each evening and she has to be very organized to keep her own household running smoothly and her family happy.

While her weekdays are long, her weekends are her own. Most Saturday mornings she packs up the family — including dog, cat and dove! — and leaves Paris to head out to their country home, often hauling along some flowers for the ride because their presence is second nature to her. Her son, Achille, sometimes brings a friend, and her daughter, Iris, comes to spend the time with her horse in livery in the country.

At her charming country house there is an immediate change in rhythm. Clarisse will tend the garden, of course, but it is carefully planted and designed so as not to be too labor intensive. Her husband, Jerome, is an architect, and they regularly update their house, doing much of the work themselves. There is no rush to get work done; planning a renovation together, pooling and discussing ideas and adapting their plans to what can be realistically achieved, is part of their shared leisure time, a creative activity "à deux."

For Clarisse and her family, this is a retreat, a haven of peace with its view over the fields and its gentle forms and colors of the old house and barns. This is the time when they can prepare meals together, talk about their week, read a good book in the shade of a tree. During this time Clarisse can relax and store up the energy she'll need for another week creating some of the most poetic flower arrangements in Paris.

Clarisse always arrives from Paris with some flowers for the house, simple country-style blooms that fit well in this rural setting. Their colors find an echo in the lime-green touches of the sitting room.

This is the country, there is nothing too precious in the decor, inside the weekend house the furniture is simple and the mood is relaxed.

The pretty 19th-century cottage is typical of the local architecture. The garden
is elegant and perfect for country-style
entertaining.

94

CORNÉLIE

Running several households to perfection, keeping a large family ticking and happy, and working as an interior designer requires some levelheaded organizational skills.

Cornélie is one of those girls who appear to have it all: several stunning homes, gorgeous children, a loving husband. Added to that, she is delightfully down-to-earth, a good friend and a reliable mother.

Her children are adults at the outset of their professional lives now, but they often come home for the weekend and Cornélie is still at the heart of family life. "I'm lucky," she laughs, "the parties are always around my table!"

She continues to organize the family holidays and make sure that wherever they meet, everything is ready and welcoming. Winters are spent in Paris, July in Cabourg, and the rest of the summer in Cap Ferret. It is an art to make each house feel like home, to give each place a clear identity, with an instantly familiar style.

One of six girls, Cornélie is used to busy family life. She is close to her sisters and they often share shopping trips and family holidays. Christmas each year sees them all reunited in Provence, when the sisters, with their respective husbands and children, join the grandparents for a very traditional celebration. "I love our huge Christmas. There is a giant tree, a traditional festive meal and enough place to seat the thirty or so members of the family. It's never a very quiet affair!"

Her husband, Stanis, is a busy man, but they share many interests and weekends are spent together, often at the St. Ouen flea markets looking for exceptional antiques or new designers at their favorite markets, Serpette and Paul Bert. These outings are often followed by a late lunch with friends at the current de rigueur restaurant, Ma Cocotte.

They travel a great deal and in particular both enjoy safaris. For Stanis it is the wildlife that draws him, the great outdoors. Cornélie is happy to accompany him and loves to explore the local culture, always on the lookout for new design ideas.

The modern art they both adore makes a statement in their contemporary interiors. Huge photos enlarged to take up a whole wall, sections of street art framed beneath Plexiglas, or more traditional paintings fill their various homes. Cornélie likes to support budding talent and loves to buy from new artists.

An important part of Cornélie's discipline is her daily ride. Her horse, Lescure, is in livery at the Paris Polo Club, but when she goes out to spend time at her beach house near Cabourg on the Normandy Coast, he often comes in a horse van behind her car. Long gallops along the sandy beaches are as much of a pleasure for the mount as for the cavalier.

Cabourg has always been a favorite destination in July for Stanis and Cornélie. It's only a couple of hours from Paris but is a wonderful playground for the whole family and a guaranteed breath of fresh air. Their large modern home faces the Atlantic, with only the dunes between them and the water's edge.

Late summer is spent enjoying the social whirlwind of Cap Ferret, entertaining and being entertained.

Cornélie's Paris house is within easy reach of the 16th arrondissement, with its chic cafés and opportunities to shop.

The manicured garden and imposing facade of the house make a bold statement, a style that is continued once inside.

Cornélie's favorite pieces of street art are perfectly at home in her contemporary interiors.

In each of her homes, Cornélie's sure eye for interior design has produced a signature style of clean, bold lines and statement furniture that draws admiration among friends.

With her children growing up, Cornélie found herself with more time on her hands and was looking for a way to reinvent herself. Friends asked her for advice on their interiors, so gradually she started taking on complete makeovers. Today she is often asked to help with a friend's beach house or Parisian apartment. She also decorated her children's first homes. As a result, her order book is full, and if we meet for lunch, it is not unusual to make a detour: "I just need to check out a new address; I think they may have the fabric I need for that project I told you about."

Cornélie lives a comfortable life; there is no denying that. Through her talent for design and her outgoing nature, she has avoided the dangers of the empty nester, and today she has no trouble keeping herself busy and her family content.

The main bedroom on the upper floor is furnished in elegant and muted tones.

The kitchen design is sleek and practical. With a large family to feed, the traditional stove takes pride of place.

Family dining takes place here, adjacent to the kitchen, at a long table with cane chairs in various shades picked from the colors in the room.

Cornélie loves to ride Lescure each day. He is big and powerful, but their mutual trust is evident.

EVELYNE

E velyne's life runs to the rhythm of the grapevines and their seasons, as did the lives of her parents, and their parents, and their parents and grandparents before them. Because Evelyne and her husband are the fifth generation of the same family to produce Boizel champagne.

I was first connected with Evelyne by a mutual friend who had described Evelyne's passion for life and her interesting work. I made contact and we met for lunch in a little *bistrot* in the 9th arrondissement. When I arrived she was already at our table. The first thing I noticed about Evelyne was her warm smile and the sparkle in her eyes: she is a born communicator, always eager to meet new people.

We chatted easily for nearly three hours. I was fascinated by the insight she so generously gave me into her very traditional world and by her natural modesty, despite her many achievements. Since that day, whenever we meet, it is always with the same pleasure, always with plenty to share and discuss.

Creating fine champagne is a meticulous business. It requires mixing centuries-old traditions with modern-day marketing and innovation. It is an industry that has to remain true to its time-honored techniques, yet can no longer survive without using today's marketing and communication tools. This juxtaposition is mirrored in Evelyne's own lifestyle: while she lives a very traditional French life, she loves keeping up with anything new.

Evelyne and her husband, Christophe, were not originally destined to the family business. Boizel has always been passed down from father to son, but the premature deaths of her father and her older brother pushed Evelyne unexpectedly to the top of the family hierarchy, and she and Christophe became responsible for the continuation of her family name.

At the time, Evelyne was studying art and Christophe had just started his career as an engineer. They were still very young for such heavy responsibility, but they felt strongly that the family business had to be continued and threw themselves wholeheartedly into their new roles.

Today, forty years later, their hard work and continually imaginative management has brought Boizel champagne firmly into the 21st century.

Being at the head of a traditional company meant they both needed to know how to manage every aspect of the business. But as time has passed, individual specialties and preferences have formed quite naturally. While Christophe takes charge of the blending of the grapes for each new production, Evelyne has embraced the role of marketing her company and of curating its public image.

She is unafraid of learning new technologies. When they decided to merge with other champagne producers and float the company on the stock exchange, Evelyne headed the negotiations. She launched one of the first Internet sites to sell champagne and it was Evelyne who had the idea of marketing a special bottle for Christmas each year and inviting a well-known artist or designer to create the label.

This creativity and dynamism keeps Evelyne very busy as she travels the world representing the family name.

There are reminders
of the family history at
every corner.

Of course, Evelyne is not only a businesswoman but also a loving wife, mother and grandmother. She is proud to be the fifth generation of her family to produce the champagne, but even more proud to hand the company down to the sixth generation and to see the seventh already on its way.

While she may be looking forward to the next generation, Evelyne continues to honor her family's past. The family archives are rich and well documented. Each generation of the family had their own personalities and individual talents; their photos and paperwork are testament to that. And there are other souvenirs: charming handwritten documents, wine cellar records, old labels from bottles, stencils used for barrels — all elements that were useful to Evelyne when she came to write a book of her family's history.

In keeping with her role as the link between past and present in her own family, her home is an impressive, historic 19th-century property whose wide entrance opens onto one of the main streets of her 21st-century town. It is only a short drive from the family champagne cellars. She and Christophe bought the house from family friends and raised their children here.

Evelyne's style is quite classical and elegant, and her home is decorated beautifully with pieces of contemporary art dotted here and there alongside antique furniture and elegant fabrics.

Given the proximity to town, Evelyne can leave the house for errands on foot — something she loves. Basket in hand, she makes the short walk to her preferred *boulangerie*, butcher, farmers market or fishmonger. In typical French manner, Evelyne finds time to shop each day and is faithful to her favorite tradesmen, preferring to buy her baguette in one boulangerie but her macarons in another.

She loves to entertain and to lay a beautiful table. She learned this from her mother and grandmother. I suppose it is not surprising that a lady so steeped in the tradition of champagne production should know all there is about laying a fine table and the etiquette involved.

The art of fine living is just one of the many things that Evelyne will take pleasure in passing down to her grandchildren. She will also ensure that though they are growing up in the modern world, they will treasure the direct link to another era that is safely tucked away in the family genes.

Evelyne and Christophe inspect the grapes on a gently sloping vineyard above their town.

The family history is carefully documented with photos and historical records.

The elegant proportions of their home are the perfect setting for their mix of antiques and comfortable furniture.

In the salon, the original wood paneling frames the fireplace and lends a beautiful symmetry to the room.

The dining room is spacious, and Evelyne enjoys setting the table here for dinner with friends.

The home is set in the town center, so the garden is walled on all sides and is bordered with beautiful flowerbeds.

FRÉDÉRIQUE

My great friend Frédérique is forever on the go. She tells me, "The only time I sit down is in the car!" Even so, when she is in her car she has her diary open on the seat beside her, making and changing appointments as she goes through her day. At home, merely walking around checking her horses in the paddocks gives her several kilometers of brisk walking each day, but that is not enough for her.

Frédérique's daily routine starts early. She's up at around six o'clock and continues through the day at a rapid pace. Once she has driven her children to school and done her daily shopping, she returns to do the paddock rounds. This is her favorite moment and she relishes feeding the horses and checking up on each and every one. As she so sweetly puts it, "I like to see if they've slept well."

Raising horses has always been Fred's dream. Once she had the space, she set about finding a couple of brood mares and tracking down the most suitable sires.

At least one morning a week we ride together. In the afternoons after our rides I prefer to take things easy: ride home at a slow pace, take care of my horse, and gently walk him back to pasture before getting on with some quiet work while enjoying that lovely feeling of having exercised well.

Fred, on the other hand, will finish the ride, load her horse into her van, drive home, tend to her mount, quickly shower and change, and then join other friends for lunch and a game of tennis.

As I said, it is hard to keep up. But this just adds to Frédérique's charm because it makes her so much fun. Fred is full of a contagious enthusiasm and is game for anything you may suggest. Living the high life is actually in her blood: she is a direct descendant of the Montgolfier family, famous for inventing the hot air balloon.

As well as riding and playing tennis, Frédérique competes in marathons and triathlons. She trains with a deceiving nonchalance that conceals her competitive spirit. She and her husband Arnaud firmly believe in the importance of sports and have encouraged their children, Stanislas and Charlotte, to compete regularly, be it in the show jumping arena or on the rugby field.

Her wise *maman* taught Fred to be meticulous. She is always impeccably turned out: perfect hair, perfect nails, pristine clothing — even her riding boots are spotless. She carries this attention to detail beyond her own person, as I can testify. Within minutes of seeing her, she will re-button a jacket I'm wearing, or walk into my house and straighten the cushions, simply out of habit.

Before moving to Normandy, she and Arnaud first lived in Paris, pursuing successful careers in advertising. Their Parisian life was busy and never boring, but they both dreamed of a sprawling property in the country.

117

The daily routine includes taking care of her horses, maintaining the stables. Hopefully the prizes will follow.

Fred and her daughter, Charlotte, walk through the grounds of the château to the outdoor arena for a workout before the next day's jumping competition.

Arnaud is extremely pragmatic. He knew they'd enjoy the space that came with a chateau but was determined to choose a property that could pay for its own keep. They settled on the chateau d'Emalleville because the two symmetrical wings were already renovated as guest rooms, and there were plenty of other outbuildings for hosting larger events. They decided to set up business as a luxury bed and breakfast venue.

In the late '90s they moved in, redecorated the guest wings and a couple of months later opened their chateau B&B for business. Within a short time they became one of the best addresses in our part of Normandy and were welcoming visitors from all over the world.

Of course, maintaining the chateau and grounds demands a lot of work and organization; Fred makes sure that the guest rooms run smoothly. But she is more of an outdoor girl than one who spends time on interior design or in the kitchen. If you ask her what she thinks of living in a chateau, she'll reply in her habitually candid manner that she likes having the paddocks for her horses, but would be just as happy in a small house.

Besides running the chateau B&B, Arnaud and Fred also completely renovated the 18th-century greenhouse in the park and planted hundreds of fruit trees, roses and hydrangeas. This makes

for a lot of fruit, and in the month of May I always get calls from Fred: "Do you want to come and pick some cherries? We can't possible eat them all!" Or, "Would you like a basket of plums? We have way too many!" All through the summer, in typical French fashion, they make jams and jellies for themselves and for their guests' breakfasts.

For a French woman Fred has an amazing appetite. Never shy to eat dessert or enjoy a glass or two of wine, she loves receiving dinner invites but hates to cook. Luckily, for her own dinner parties she can rely on her housekeeper to prepare the meal.

In the French countryside, entertaining at home is in our blood, and in their lovely home Fred and Arnaud enjoy a busy social life. In the summer they lay dinner tables in the garden beneath a huge beech tree, and in early January they are known for their open house, where friends are welcome throughout the afternoon and early evening to share champagne, eat the traditional *galette des rois* and toast the New Year in.

So if one day you're lucky enough to stay at Emalleville, and if you manage to squeeze a chat into Frédérique's hectic schedule, then bear in mind all I've told you about her busy days. With this insider's knowledge you'll be even more delighted by her hospitality, energy, and *joie de vivre.*"

The broad staircase and wide windows allow light to stream into the heart of the chateau.

An 18th-century trumeau with its original mirror sits over the marble fireplace in the salon.

The setting may be grand, but the simple details make this a real family home.

Family meals are taken in the kitchen, but when friends or guests are invited to dinner, Fred prepares the long table in the dining room.

Living in a beautiful chateau is both a privilege and a responsibility. The whole family takes pride in the impeccable maintenance of the beautiful grounds.

LAURE

When I visited Laure in her beautiful home down a leafy cul-de-sac in Paris, she apologized for bringing me over to the not-quite-so-fashionable 15th arrondissement! "Why do you apologize?" I asked. "This is divine!" Laure lives in a building that was formerly an artist's studio. In fact, the whole street was used by artists and must have been a lively little *quartier* at the beginning of the century. Today, each house has been renovated and the result is a series of chic, upbeat designer homes, each three stories high.

Renovating and redecorating homes is nothing new to Laure. She and her husband, Bertrand, have renovated six homes since they were married, gradually climbing the property ladder with their talent for contemporary interiors and sure eye for architectural design.

After training in art school, Laure worked in a Parisian auction house, where she learned about the antique trade, perfected her eye for detail and met Bertrand. Watching chairs, paintings and silverware go under the hammer was a fantastic lesson in the history of design. This was Laure's chance to understand how trends evolve, how tastes develop and how contemporary innovation is always influenced by historical reference.

She started buying the unwanted pieces from the auction house and bringing them home to add patina and character before selling them on. As her style developed, so did her popularity and her clientele, and fresh material was required. Bertrand accompanied her on weekend shopping expeditions: from *brocante* fairs and flea markets, Laure hauled her treasures home to embellish and repurpose.

She grew more and more interested in the intricate designs of botanical diagrams and illustrations from 18th-century curiosity cabinets and the 19th-century graphics found in old books, bills of purchase or printed notices. Today Laure hunts down these sorts of materials in the specialized old book flea market on the Square Georges Brassens, near her home, each Sunday morning.

Drawing on her art training, she reworked the old illustrations and gave them a modern twist, mixing them together with eclectic graphics to produce a range of designs with a recognizable style. In 2005 when she showed her vintage furniture and print designs at the famous Paris Maison et Objet salon, her graphics were an overnight success. A year on, Maison Caumont was born and she had her own complete line of wallpapers and fabrics.

Meanwhile Laure and Bertrand's everyday Parisian life continued, with a family to keep happy. Laure is a true Parisian, and although now and again she dreams of living in the country, she knows that she would miss Paris too much. She loves the proximity of the little restaurants, she loves going to the theater in the evening, and she loves shopping at her favorite addresses.

At eighteen years old, her eldest daughter, Marie, is fast becoming independent, but her youngest girl, Blanche, is only eleven and loves to accompany Laure to exhibitions and craft fairs. Although still young, she has very clear ideas about design and has her own sewing machine in her bedroom, where she works on her own creations.

Their third child, César, is still taken to school each morning by Laure or Bertrand, and if they finish their own work late in the

Laure enjoys the luxury of working from an office at home. Here she can perfect her designs, experiment with new ideas and stay in touch with clients all around the world.

Samples of her designs are displayed against the bold colors of her home décor. Fabric prototypes sit alongside samples of wallpaper.

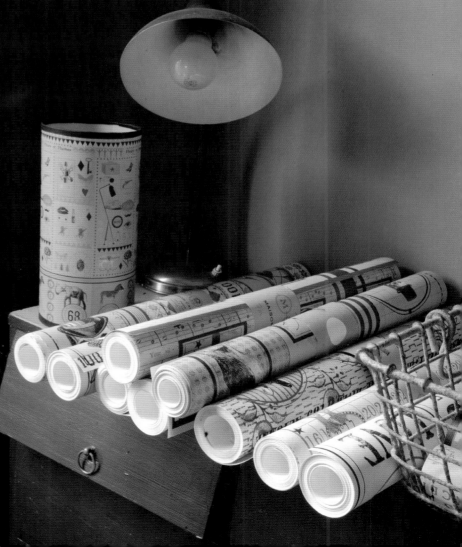

evening, he'll stay longer at school or spend time with his favorite child minder. This is all part of living in the city, juggling family and professional lives.

Laure loves to cook and in true Parisian style shops at a great food market. There is a family tradition of brunch at their house every Sunday. Laure buys fresh food at the open-air market every Sunday morning. Friends arrive at half past one and the brunch continues through the afternoon. Their weekly brunch is a great way for the parents to relax and enjoy each other's company while all the children play in the house or cycle up and down the little impasse.

The family has regular tastes of country life at their summerhouse on the Ile d'Oleron on the Atlantic Coast. Here Laure has decorated her country house in her signature style, a mix of vintage, antique and industrial-style furniture, with her muted palette of colors and bold graphic designs on the walls. On Oleron, life moves at more leisurely pace. A lot of time is spent with friends and the children discover the delights of bare feet on sand, catching crabs in rock pools and cycling instead of using the car.

Often their visits make Laure wonder if they should move there permanently, if they should leave the capital and opt for a quieter life by the sea, but each time her beloved Paris calls her back.

Laure and Bertrand are a Parisian couple on the move: creative, dynamic and determined to enjoy life *à la française*. The country will be the right place to be one day, but for now Paris is their home.

The charming impasse was once home to Parisian artists. Today the studios have become family homes, but the artistic influence can still be seen.

Mid-century vintage furniture is a perfect style for Laure's comfortable family home.

Tableware is stored within easy reach behind huge antique doors that run the length of the dining room wall.

Details from the family bedrooms and the children's bathroom show how art is omnipresent.

The bedrooms still have their original fireplace surrounds, which now serve as frames to Laure's vignettes.

MARIE-CHRISTINE

The open-air markets in Provence are more than just a place to buy food or a pretty basket; they are a sensorial experience, an invitation to eat well and enjoy life.

One Saturday morning, while staying with friends in the South, we went to the local market for the weekend shopping. I bought melons and peaches before becoming completely side-tracked by some olives and cheese. By then, it was time to go looking for my friends.

Our meet-up point was the café by the village fountain, where everyone stops for a break after filling their shopping baskets. Sure enough, I found my friends sitting in the shade at an extended table that was full of laughter and animated discussion. This is where I met Marie-Christine for the first time. She was at the center of the table, laughing as her husband Louis joked about how she was trying to persuade him to get another dog.

I sat down, a coffee appearing in front of me, and listened to the rest of the conversation. I quickly understood that Marie-Christine and Louis were the owners of the beautiful chateau on the hill above my friend's house whose restoration work I had heard so much about. By the time the coffees were finished, Marie-Christine and Louis had invited us for lunch the next day. I could hardly wait!

The following morning the sun was shining, the cicadas were singing, and at noon we made our way to Marie-Christine's home. As we drove through the chateau's wide gates and parked the car, my friend nudged me and said with a smile, *"Ma chérie,* you are going to love this!"

Louis heard our car arrive and as we walked towards the front of the chateau he swung the huge door open to greet us, revealing the enormous entrance hall with its oversized chandelier. It took my breath away. Louis saw me looking up at the pretty crystal tears hanging from their ornate luster frame and said laughing, "The antique dealer had to sell it to us. It was too big for anybody else's home!"

The house seemed to be bathed in a gentle light, an impression reinforced by the soft color of the stone floor and staircase, and the patina on the walls. My eye was drawn to the next room and to the door on the other side, which opened to a view over the terrace where I could see Marie-Christine adding flowers to her table.

We walked through the house and out to the terrace, as if drawn by a magnet. There were small tables and chairs beneath a large tree on the left, and large, wide steps leading down to the lawn. Marie-Christine came to welcome us. *"Bonjour,* welcome. Look what lovely weather we have. Come this way." Cheeks were kissed; compliments paid — *"mais tu es très chic aujourd'hui,"* "merci ma chérie, et toi toujours aussi belle"* — chairs taken into the shade. Champagne corks popped, and we drank a glass or two of bubbles and chatted about this and that until lunch commenced.

The next couple of hours sped by as our wonderfully lazy Mediterranean lunch was punctuated by *"c'est delicieux,"* "have some more of this," *"merci, c'est merveilleux, c'est exquis."* Throughout the meal, I kept looking at the façade of the chateau and its fantastic view, thinking what an amazing project it would be for anyone, let alone a couple on the verge of retirement. After lunch Marie-Christine invited me to take a tour of the chateau. As we wandered she told me the astounding story of how they came to be here.

Marie-Christine and Louis park their car and then walk through the little town to the market square, baskets in hand, with their dog Gatsby leading the way.

Market day in Provence is rich in color and perfume. Vendors compete to attract clients to their stands with attractively arranged food, herbs or handmade soaps. Coffee with friends after the shopping is done is all part of the weekly ritual.

The more she told me about their ten-year renovation project the more I was struck by her modesty. There was no trace of affectation as she led me from one room to another; rather, she was simply filled with the enjoyment of sharing a work of art. At moments I even wondered if she was aware of the scale and beauty of the work she and Louis have achieved.

Nothing had prepared them for this project. Louis owned a garage in Nice and Marie-Christine had worked for twenty years as a stylist in the south of France, in particular for the magazine *Côté Sud*. They had built their own home in Nice but had never before attempted to rescue a dilapidated 17th-century chateau.

With Louis's imminent retirement, they were looking to leave Nice and find a house in the country. Marie-Christine still worked a little, but she longed to create a country home for the two of them, somewhere to receive friends, to have their daughter come for visits, maybe one day have their grandchildren stay.

They dreamed of a wonderful view, an old stone building and a country setting. They only visited the chateau de Moissac out of curiosity, not with the intention to buy; 4,900 square feet was way bigger than they required, and the chateau was on the edge of a village, when they hoped for a more remote setting in the countryside.

Their first impression should have put them off. Half the roof was gone and a tree was growing inside the entrance; the staircase was missing; the doors had been ransacked, and not only had the windows been removed but the openings were bricked up.

And yet, despite all of this, Marie-Christine could see herself here, in this 17th-century building, formerly home to Provençal nobility. Despite the extensive damage, she could already envision the building restored, repaired and brought back to life.

Louis is happy when his wife is happy. Faced with her enthusiasm he began to think seriously about the feasibility of the huge project. Once he started researching the history of the place and began to hunt for possible sources for replacement doors, shutters, fireplaces, even roof tiles, he was hooked on the idea.

Louis and Marie-Christine worked side by side on the project. He took care of the technical and practical aspects, but it was her sure eye that guided their decisions.

As the restoration progressed, the couple formed a clearer picture of how the chateau could be used. Her years of experience in the styling and decoration business made her sure that the chateau could provide the perfect setting for photo shoots and small events. The decision was made to turn the chateau over to the visual arts, to make it a place where photographers and stylists could let their imaginations roam free.

With the remodel complete, today this idea has become a reality. Marie-Christine enjoys the prolonged contact with a profession that she loved so much, added to which she appreciates that she is now working from home on a project that she created from scratch.

Their own living space is on the ground floor. Marie-Christine wanted a large salon with big white sofas. This is a place to be comfortable and it is close to the huge kitchen with its open fireplace and wide range. There are several back kitchens close by, and on the other side of the entrance halls a bedroom for themselves, with a smaller room next door for their granddaughter, who often comes to stay at the weekend. On the next two floors is a series of sparsely but beautifully furnished bedrooms and bathrooms, allowing stylists to use the space to their own advantage.

The result is simply breathtaking. There is not one detail that isn't perfectly in line with the age and style of the chateau. Every room has been entirely refurbished, from the chapel in the cellar to the former maids' rooms at the top of the house.

It is as if all these years of styling were preparing Marie-Christine for the day when she would meet this chateau, as if she were the one who could unlock the beauty in its walls, re-create the perfect patina, and furnish it in a way that resonates best with its Provençal setting.

It is hard to believe that the chateau was once in ruins. Today every wall, every room, every tiny detail has been exquisitely renovated and the building has been brought back to life.

Seen from a distance, perched on a hill over its own vine-yards, the chateau is calm and imposing; an impression that is reinforced once you walk through the doors and soak in the restrained, poised décor.

The chateau may be grand, but Marie-Christine's sure eye has created elegant rooms for everyday living. Here the salon is comfortable but never cluttered. Contemporary pieces are mixed with antique furniture, and the soft palette is easy on the eye.

The kitchen has a handsome arched ceiling and a wide-open fireplace, which is used daily during the winter months. The long farm table sits beneath a crystal chandelier; linens and tableware in neutrals blend into the overall color scheme.

The exceptionally high ceilings make the large bedrooms feel even more so. The walls are plastered using traditional techniques and colors, complementing the old tile floors.

Furniture and fittings are chosen for their quality and design. Marie-Christine prefers sparse furnishings highlighted with small authentic details.

MARIE

For Marie, a wire sculptor, the only daughter of an architect and wife of a furniture designer, design and shape are an essential part of life.

Tall and slim with long legs, Marie moves like a ballet dancer, as lithe and flexible as the wire that she so artfully bends into her sculptures. With her couture wardrobe and perfect figure, she is the archetype of the chic French girl, equally nonchalant and elegant in a pair of jeans as in a designer dress and stilettos.

Marie loves to dress well; it is something she adores. Her regular trips to Paris are moments when she indulges her chic Parisian couture side. Her little jewel of a pied-à-terre apartment in Paris is ideal for business appointments but also perfectly placed for shopping sprees and lunches with friends.

At her home in the country, Marie dresses casually in jeans and a t-shirt or a silk shirt; comfort meets style for her family life. Despite her simple daily attire, her feminine fashion stands out all the more because she's the only girl in the house — in addition to her husband and two sons, even the dog is a boy! But being the only girl has its perks: Marie's husband Emmanuel has a strong Gallic personality and is fiercely proud of his gorgeous and talented wife, and her two lovely boys dote on their *maman*.

Family life runs to a simple routine: the boys go to school in the nearby town, and after she has dropped them off, she'll often stop at the market on the central square before heading home for a day of creating. Marie and Emmanuel both work from their respective offices at home. They are conscientious about balancing work, family, and the restoration of their recently purchased home.

In the early years of their married life, Marie and Emmanuel lived in the north of Paris, but he comes from the southwest of France and his roots were calling him home. He persuaded Marie to move down as far as Toulouse for a couple of years before taking her one step farther, when they bought the vast *bastide* that they are in the process of restoring.

Their home lies in its own grounds of many acres, alongside cedar trees that were planted when the house was built nearly 200 years ago. When they bought the property, it had stood empty for twenty-five years. The first time they toured the house and barns, Marie just laughed, "But it's way too big for us!"

Inside all the electricity and plumbing needed to be rethought, rooms remodeled and decorated, and light allowed inside. The façade of the house also needed attention, but the bones and foundation were good and the natural grace of the building and various barns and annexes were something Marie and Emmanuel admired and respected.

Emmanuel was aware that he was asking a lot of his chic town mouse; moving from a busy city with its many forms of entertainment, to an isolated property surrounded by fields was sure to be a shock. But they both threw themselves wholeheartedly into the remodeling of the house. Wherever they renovated, they did it in style as befits a design couple.

In the midst of this dusty makeover, Marie's walk-in closet was completed in record time, a concession to her femininity and a refuge on days when the building site was a little too much to handle. The house décor is punctuated in the bold, bright colors that Marie

The strong bones of the old house are accentuated by bold interior design, making the most of the natural light and contrasting blocks of bright color – in particular in Marie's dressing room, where her stylish wardrobe hangs against a backdrop of yellow walls.

As renovation indoors is nearly completed, the couple will make decisions on how best to restore the exterior of the bastide. The art of good renovating is to overhaul without losing the essential character of the house.

loves so much. Her personal dressing room is beautifully ordered and color blocked. Her bright silk shirts hang in line, and her high heels are perched on a shelf, waiting for their next outing to Paris.

This love of color is reflected in her work too. The simple grey lines of the wire sculptures are enhanced with bright beads that she sources in the ceramic capital of the south of France, the little town of Vallauris.

Marie started creating her wire structures as a base for sculptures made of plaster. The wire was meant as a support for the heavy outer structure, but she quickly realized that it was this wire support that she found the most interesting. She loved the way the wire allowed her to create large sculptures that are extremely light, and she gradually improved her techniques until she was able to fashion practically any object, no matter how detailed.

One of the pleasant realities of living in the country is that there are few distractions. Marie's working day is generally uninterrupted, allowing her to take on larger orders. She worried that producing series of sculptures may lessen the artistic value of her creations, but as a counterweight, she also produces one-off pieces for gallery shows on both sides of the Atlantic.

Her address book is impressive. She seems to have friends in every couture house of Paris and her work is associated with the most prestigious names. Her chandeliers hang in the boutiques of Monsieur Dior, her wire bicycle took center stage in the window of the iconic Paris store Colette, and Roger Vivier's shoe boutique windows have long been decorated by Marie. In fact, her first really big break came when the artistic director of Hermès commissioned four life-size horses, represented at full gallop, for their store in Los Angeles.

For the chic Marie, who loves to shop and who adores the buzz of the city, it took a while to learn how to live in the country. Today there is no doubt that she has grown to appreciate the luxury of space that her country house affords and the beautiful sunlight of the south. And now after each excursion to Paris or to Toulouse she looks forward to returning to the tranquility of a 19th-century property that she can truly call home.

The room where Marie creates looks more like an office than a working studio. She is a tidy artist, and finished pieces are displayed around the room, while she works on new projects at a table in the center.

All artists likes to sign their work, and Marie is no exception. Here a signature is ready to take its place on a lamp base.

NATHALIE

Nathalie's tale is one of renewal, of re-creation, and of starting afresh.

Making new from old is a theme that permeates every area of her life, be it in her original training in art restoration; her exquisite sculptures born from scraps of discarded bark and seeds; the garden she has helped create from an empty field; the loving relationship she has formed with her second husband, when they each found themselves unexpectedly alone; or the clean, modern living space she has designed in the former stable block of her husband's 16th-century manor house.

Nathalie divides her time between Paris and the family property in La Sarthe, a region about three hours' drive from my home in Normandy. Her country retreat lies outside a tiny old stone village, but she can be tracked down by following the signs for her *jardin remarquable*. In France, this award is given to gardens that are worth the detour for their historical and botanical interest, their creative design and impeccable maintenance.

And it is a detour. The narrow lane leads from the village through fields until the vista opens up to an imposing stone gateway and a long, straight drive with an austere stone edifice at the end. The visitor makes his way up the drive, not knowing whether to admire the handsome white cows in the fields on the left, the bowers of roses on the right, or the enormous yew topiaries that frame the manor house at the top of the driveway.

Nathalie greets guests warmly even if they are first-time visitors merely wishing to tour the gardens. One day I arrived at her home with friends early in the morning. Before getting our feet wet on the dew-sodden lawn, we were ushered inside for tea, coffee and tartines of fresh bread and homemade jam.

And then with the brisk command, "Off we go; we mustn't miss this wonderful light," Nathalie commenced her tour of the gardens, explaining how they came to be and at the same time telling her own life story.

Her husband, Thibault de Reimpré, and his first wife, Isabelle, with whom Nathalie was a close friend, originally created the gardens of Le Mirail from scratch. At that time, Nathalie knew little about plants and their care, but Isabelle encouraged her to become involved with the garden and its maintenance.

Nathalie had trained as an expert in art restoration and had worked on the masterpieces stored in the Palace of Versailles; but getting her hands covered in earth and her feet wet was a new experience to her.

As she became more involved in the garden, she also grew closer to Isabelle and Thibault, and supported Thibault when Isabelle lost her fight against cancer. In the following years, companionship grew into love; being divorced and with three grown children, Nathalie found herself drawn into a new relationship with a man who was already a friend and with whom she had shared passions for both gardening and art.

From the spring on through to the autumn, the garden is open to the public. The effects of this are twofold: there is a certain pressure to keep the grounds in immaculate condition, whatever the weather, but also there is the pleasure of meeting other passionate gardeners, eager to share and learn from the work accomplished at Le Mirail.

159

A small summerhouse with climbing rose sits at the end of the lawn and provides a viewpoint up to the imposing manor house.

Giant Yew topiaries stand like sentinels along the drive, expertly clipped to the same size but not identical in shape – simple elegance.

Structure in a large garden is all-important. The space is carefully divided and interrupted to create points of interest and settings for favorite plants.

As the sun rises behind the manor house, the beauty of the shaped hedges is revealed in the play of shadows and light.

Because designing a garden of this proportion is much more than just combining colors; winters are spent planning, transplanting, and pruning, reshaping and dreaming. With the arrival of spring each year comes the assessment of the winter's work: has the garden's space been judiciously shaped to invite visitors to explore, to stimulate their curiosity and to reward their eye? Was that rose cut back hard enough? Is the view up to the house tranquil and unencumbered? Does the new water feature, with Nathalie's sculpture positioned at one end, lead the eye out to the valley beyond?

Once the structural winter work in the garden is complete, Nathalie and Thibault each retire to their painting studios and release their artistic energies in a different direction. The green paths and borders of the garden make way for canvases pulled taut over wooden *châssis* (stretchers). Nathalie loves this element of contrast in their lives: working one minute on a classical garden and the next on contemporary and often abstract art.

Nathalie and her husband are both passionate artists. They each understand the need to open up to the world around, but also to have more reclusive periods of reflection and contemplation. They recognize each other's need for private space, and the result is a loving relationship based on mutual respect and admiration. Nathalie has often told me that Thibault's love makes her free. What greater compliment could there be?

Consequently, while Nathalie's summers are spent outdoors, enjoying open vistas and wide horizons, her winters are more solitary, with much time spent alone indoors creating her sculptures and painting at her easel. This peaceful time is the season for meditation, for using the artistic energy stored up over the summer months and remaining in close communion with nature.

Besides her beautiful canvases, which are painted from memory, Nathalie also assembles intricate sculptures, surprising imitations of insects reminiscent of the collections of 19th-century botanists and explorers. She collects oriental and primitive art, and their exotic influences are clearly seen in her sculptures.

Nathalie has always loved to travel. Her sketches and watercolors fill a shelf of beautiful travel journals. Pages of inks and watercolors capture trees, landscapes, fountains and sea fronts, visual notes and *aide-mémoires*.

The manor house is comfortable during the summer months, but in winter the stone walls and high ceilings make it more difficult to heat. With so much time spent indoors during the winter months, Thibault suggested that Nathalie design a new living space for them in the former stable block. Here Nathalie was able to create a space that reflected her own aesthetics and mark a fresh start for the new couple.

The new room is flooded with light and filled with the warmth of the sunshine streaming in through the windows. It is impossible not to feel at ease in this space. Besides their bedroom and bathroom, nearly all the remaining space is one large open area, which naturally moves from sitting room to art studio, to showroom to kitchen to workshop.

Nathalie chose a central modern staircase, which opens up to a guest room and a viewing gallery, without obscuring any parts of the space below. It is from here that she and Thibault can appraise their canvases laid out on the floor beneath.

She paints for her pleasure and shows at small local exhibitions. But her work is also sold in a gallery in the Perigord region of southwest France, and her paintings are sent around the world.

Part of each month is spent in Paris, where Nathalie and Thibault have a very different routine from their country habits, and she enjoys the contrast between the two. In Paris, they live in an old apartment with a huge atelier boasting windows two stories high, allowing light to flood into the room. Here the days are filled with Parisian friends and family, shopping at a favorite store or two, or visiting an exhibition.

Nathalie's life is full of contrasts: working on a classical garden but creating modern art; enjoying a busy life in Paris and a slower pace in the country; moments of sharing and then time to be alone. Yet in both places, she feels at home, at ease, and fulfilled.

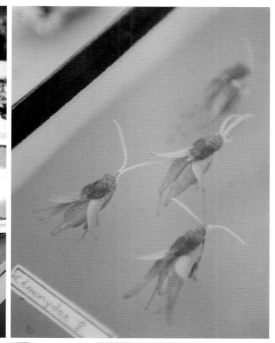

During the winter, when more time is spent indoors, Nathalie works on her painting and sculpture. Her large canvases are created from memory and with the help of her visual notes made in travel journals.

To create her unusual sculptures, she collects pieces of wood, seed pods, feathers, even bones. These elements collected locally or brought back from trips abroad, once assembled can give the illusion of a small animal or insect.

Nathalie designed their spacious home as an open plan. Areas of the large room are used for specific purposes, but there are no dividing walls, and the freedom of movement from salon to studio to kitchen creates a very relaxed and comfortable atmosphere.

SABINE

While on holiday in the south of France, a friend asked me to come for a drive: "There's a lady you should meet. I'm sure you'd like her; she has an art gallery in her garden." Never slow to accept an intriguing invitation, I packed my camera and we set off. I wondered what this little gallery would be like.

From the comfort of my friend's vintage convertible I admired the countryside as we sped through small Provençal villages and past vineyards until, finally, we turned up a long driveway and parked in the shade of an olive grove. I was already smiling. Looking toward the house there was a large crane lifting a giant stone sculpture across the roof of a barn and into the garden beyond.

We walked around the barn and down a path toward the garden. My friend exclaimed, "There she is! *Bonjour, Sabine, nous voila!*"

Sabine was a vision, almost waiflike in her white linen trousers and loose linen shirt. Looking up at the sculpture suspended in mid-air above her, she mused, "Isn't this beautiful? I love this artist's work." I mumbled something about it looking spectacular, but at the same time I was thinking that if a crane were maneuvering thirteen tons of stone into my garden, then I would look a little less serene.

As I grew to know Sabine better over the following years I realized that this is how she works; she is serene by nature. She decides what needs to be done and simply makes it happen.

On that first day, what was meant to be a quick visit spun into an entire afternoon, first spent watching the sculpture being installed and then spent touring the galleries and gardens.

Sabine and her husband, Michel, live in a house known as the Chateau Barras; it received the name when, in the 18th century, it was given as a dowry by mademoiselle Templier for her marriage to the viscount Paul de Barras, a prominent politician of the French Revolution. It is an imposing building, the walls a soft Provençal red and the shutters a pale grey. When Sabine and Michel bought the chateau, it had been on the market for a while. The country lane that ran right past the front door and divided the land in two had put off other potential buyers. Sabine and Michel made inquiries and quickly established that the local mayor would not oppose the idea of the road being diverted, thus allowing the grounds to retrieve their original design. Reassured, the couple purchased the property and set about organizing the renovation.

Inside, there was little left of the original décor except for the doors and the staircase balustrade. Painstakingly, they had floors re-laid, new windows installed and rooms repurposed until they had created the living space that suited them. The current design allows them to live comfortably *en famille* when their three children and nine grandchildren arrive for the holidays, but also allows for an atmosphere cozy enough for two when they are alone.

Once the house was completed, Sabine started work on her gallery in one of the property's stone barns. She and Michel quickly acknowledged that the initial space was too small and made the bold decision to create an extra gallery in the form of modern cube-shaped buildings in front of the barn.

Showing art, conveying beauty, is Sabine's passion. As a young

The beautiful chateau and grounds provide an ideal setting for family reunions, with enough space for quiet moments, and also space to enjoy together.

woman she trained in the Parisian Ecole du Louvre, the prestigious art school, and before moving to Barras she had owned several galleries in Paris. When she moved her home and business to the south, she had to find new contacts, establish a new clientele, and persuade existing clients back in the capital that her latest, more remote gallery was worth the trip.

My first encounter with Sabine and Michel was a very special moment for me. To observe this couple share their love of art, opening their property to the public in the hope of conveying the importance of beauty, was a lesson in humility and simplicity.

Today Sabine lives to the rhythm of her art shows. If the show itself runs during the summer months, the rest of the year is spent in preparation: choosing a theme, finding the artists, publicizing the event.

She doesn't like the term "art dealer." She prefers the concept of a passer-on of beauty, a revealer of talent. She loves to find and nurture emerging artists and takes on an almost parental role, guiding them in the works they choose to show.

Over weekends during the summer, Sabine personally receives visitors to her gallery. This is the final stage of her work. From finding the artists to explaining the works to the public, Sabine is present all along the way, and she loves this natural rhythm to the life of her gallery. "It feels like the cycle is complete, as if I accompany the art from its birth in the hands of the artist to its resting place with its new owners."

The setting for the gallery adds to its attraction, and Sabine loves her garden. The park to the chateau is enormous. Large parts of it are left as grass, but around the main house she has designed stunning parterres of Mediterranean herbs, alleys of lavender and fields of olive trees. There is also a charmingly intimate garden where gravel paths weave their way through billowing hydrangeas, rosemary bushes and roses until they lead to a gazebo, where old iron chairs and table invite visitors to sit for a while and enjoy.

A small chapel originally built for Madame de Barras stands beside the main house. For years it stood empty and open to the elements. Sabine took the project in hand: cracks in the walls were repaired, simple wooden seating was created and artists painted the walls and created stained glass windows.

The chapel renovation gave Sabine and Michel the idea of holding occasional concerts at their home, small gatherings with just a few friends. They even installed a grand piano on the terrace. These special occasions take place in the height of the summer, when evenings are warm and long and they can sit quietly beneath the chestnut tree and enjoy the music floating away into the night air.

These are the instants that mean so much to Sabine, those rare times when, as she says, "Art means life," and magic happens. What the French call *"un moment de grace."*

Sabine and Michel both savor the pleasures of life in Provence.

The hallway's soft colors are echoed in a parterre of Mediterranean herbs beyond the double doors of the entrance.

Sabine's décor is a beautiful combination of antique Provençal furniture, objects that inspire, and original artwork from artists she knows and whose work she loves.

There is room for the whole family to sit down to meals together, while the dining area is divided from the kitchen with an antique dry goods counter that has been repurposed as an island.

In a bedroom, the grey walls and curtains form a neutral backdrop for a work of art whose color is underlined by a red-velvet-upholstered antique chair.

A charming bed in a small guest room is upholstered in a Provençal-style fabric in tones that are a gentle complement to the floor tiles.

In the warm Provençal sunshine, even the cat understands the importance of a siesta in the shade.

Sabine's gallery stands to one side of the chateau and looks out over lavender bushes and olive trees.

SOPHIE

Although Sophie lives and works in the north of France, her heart is firmly anchored much further south in the wild hills of the Cévennes. Ever since she was a little girl, this has been her holiday hideaway and today there is still a home to retreat to during the summer months.

When she was growing up in Paris, her parents took the whole family to the Cévennes every August. These were long, warm days, filled with the simple pleasures of living close to nature. Sophie still remembers the old stone village they stayed in, on the side of the mountain, surrounded by tall, leafy chestnut trees.

Access to the river was on foot, in the magical company of brightly colored dragonflies and butterflies. There was a great freedom; children were left to create their own amusement, to be imaginative, to find pleasure in lazy afternoons. Berries were picked for evening desserts, games were made from beads and string, and all the while, there was a deep rumble in the background — the sound of a thousand torrents streaming down the mountainside on their way to join the deep grey rivers.

This region that started as a simple holiday base for her family is now deeply rooted into their collective soul. The attachment has seeped through the generations so that today, even Sophie's children feel the need to return regularly. Sophie's sister Lili chose to live in the Cévennes permanently, and it is her house that is the new meeting point for the clan. Her simple wooden table in the garden stretches to seat the whole family in the summer.

Sophie and Lili are close, the way sisters are meant to be. Not only do they share a love of this magical part of France, but they have real joy in spending time together. They have the same warm smile, the same slender figure: their complicity is obvious.

Sophie describes her escapades to the Cévennes as absolutely vital. Her work in the fashion and textile industry is demanding, full of deadlines and seasonal collections. She looks forward to each visit south, to getting back to nature; swimming in the icy waterfalls of the mountains; dozing in the sunshine on the flat granite rocks along the river, feeling the roar of the water beside her, her head full of the perfumes that have been familiar to her since childhood.

Being part of such a small mountain village means every neighbor has a role to play, a need to fulfill. Food is simple and sourced locally as much as possible. Everyone tends a *potager* in their garden, the vegetable beds perched on stone *restanques,* or terraces, which make the most of the high-altitude sunshine. Honey is bought from the village beekeeper and gluts of fruit from the gardens are shared among friends. The best cheese comes from the next village, ten minutes away, where a young couple take extraordinary care of a herd of goats, playing classical music to them in their barn and taking them for long walks down to the nearest river.

Knowing how much Sophie loves the freedom of this natural living, it is no surprise that as a counterbalance to her full-time work, she needed to find a way to be creative and to express herself. While working as a young stylist she started evening lessons in porcelain painting and was immediately hooked.

181

Sophie and her sister Lili prepare a charming tablescape against the backdrop of the mountain-slope garden.

The simple trestle table has seen many happy meals shared with sisters, children and cousins.

From the shady inner courtyard, to the bathroom to the romantic bedroom in the eaves, stone walls are omnipresent, a reminder of the surrounding landscape and the importance of nature in this wildly romantic setting.

ver the years, Sophie continued the porcelain painting, improving her techniques and developing her own style. She loved the sensuality of the smooth porcelain, the feel of the brush against its surface, and she learned to prepare her own colors by mixing pigments, creating subtle tones. She is gifted and her work is original. Before long she had her own atelier and her first orders for a store in Paris.

As the children grew older, she found herself alone, and this is when she met her partner, Renaud, a professional photographer. They share the same interests and are good companions. Influenced by Sophie, Renaud has also fallen under the charm of the Cévennes. Its mineral palette, tall grass, deep, dark rivers, and towering trees often figure in his black-and-white pictures.

Although she still works freelance as a fashion stylist, Sophie enjoys the balance of creating her china and working together with Renaud on photo shoots for her goods and other projects. She creates new designs to order, but the most popular remain the themes inspired by the images that fill her summer: the dragonflies that dance above the river, a group of purple violets flowering on bright green moss, insects on branches.

Today Sophie has a happy and varied lifestyle. She has found her balance between the north and the south, between work and play, and between nature and creation.

Previous Overleaf: The river plays an integral part of life in the mountains. Sophie relishes the roar of the water and the magic of the crystal clear pools where she likes to swim. Even the local goats appreciate the rocky river bed.

Sophie's work is delicate and feminine. She mixes her own pigments and takes inspiration for her designs from the dragonflies and flowers that she knows so well.

STÉPHANIE

Who would have thought it possible to experience village life in the heart of Paris? To set your watch by the chimes of the church bells; to chat with the local baker as you buy your daily bread; to watch your children go to school on foot each morning and to shop at the farmers market a few minutes from your home? Surprisingly, that is how Stéphanie and her family experience life in the 7th arrondissement of Paris.

They live on a broad avenue with a park running down the center. On summer evenings and weekends the park is the place to take a deck chair and a good book; before long you'll have a couple of friends sitting with you. This is where impromptu dinners are put together, each family bringing tables and chairs and a part of the meal. This is the place to chat with a girlfriend, to doze after a long day, to enjoy a picnic with your children — all with the stunning backdrop of Les Invalides.

Living with a view over one of the greatest monuments in Paris is a privilege that Stéphanie savors every day. She and her husband, Antoine, have raised their two children in a building that was designed by Antoine's grandfather. Their penthouse apartment is just a stone's throw from Napoleon's tomb.

It is a very special part of Paris: wide avenues, paved streets, tall imposing buildings. Everything about the *quartier* speaks of traditional living and Parisian aristocracy. Families grow up here; generations grow older on these streets but never want to leave; apartments are inherited but not sold.

Stéphanie loves this very traditional society. She is perpetuating the way she was brought up, teaching the same values to her children that she learned from her own parents.

Her warm smile and easy laughter is never fake. She loves life and her positive energy is contagious. She is as bright and happy as is her apartment with sunshine streaming in through its huge studio windows.

Social life is busy; it's easy to go out in this part of Paris. She can walk or cycle to the theater with her husband or friends, she can meet up with her children for a coffee or a snack in one of the many cafés and bistros near her home. This is a safe place to be — the neighborhood has a country club feel in the air.

Besides the proximity of good neighbors and friendly stores and cafés, Stéphanie also loves living close to their church, which stands a few blocks from her home. The church is an important part of her community. It is a place of worship of course, but also a meeting place for all in her neighborhood. Her children and her husband share her Catholic faith. Their Mass service is held every Sunday evening at 7 o'clock. The church is always packed; it is a sociable place to be and many find it reassuring to take part in the weekly ceremony surrounded by family, friends and familiar faces. "It's as if we are facing the week ahead together," says Stéphanie.

She loves to shop at the local street market, where she can buy all sorts of fresh food as well as huge bunches of cut flowers.

All along the broad avenue, penthouse apartments have big windows and balconies with ornate iron railings. Stéphanie has a privileged viewpoint over the city.

Unusually, the sitting room is twice the height of the rest of the apartment, as if to draw the visitor's gaze out through the large studio windows to the view beyond.

Stéphanie's décor is punctuated with family mementos and feminine touches.

The galley kitchen layout means that the hostess is never far from family and friends around the dining table beyond the glass partition.

A bold red has been used for the lacquered kitchen units and the facing wall. The charming painting, created by a friend, is set off in an oversized white frame.

uriously, Stéphanie's working life revolves largely around Christmas. Not for its religious meaning, but because she is the stylist and designer for many of the Christmas decorations in Paris's public places. Her background has always been in design and styling, always Parisian.

Today she's the girl who designs seven-meter high decorations for Paris's busy airports as well as the Christmas lights for the Carousel du Louvre shopping mall. She colors the city for the holidays.

Her spring and summer are spent bidding for contracts and then designing and arranging the manufacture of the huge decorative pieces. When the time finally comes to hang the decorations, it means many sleepless nights for Stéphanie, as she has to personally oversee the teams that work through the night to hang the decorations.

She loves her work and loves using her professional know-how to style events closer to home. When her daughter came of age and she and her friends were planning their debutante ball, Stéphanie was called in to style and coordinate the evening, from the invitations to the décor to the individual table settings.

Getting to know Stéphanie has been a privilege. She has given me an insight into an intimate side of Parisian living that non-native Parisians rarely have the opportunity to experience.

Stéphanie and her friends enjoy the privilege of being able to gather on the lawn in front of Les Invalides. As the sun goes down, the lights come up, highlighting the golden dome.

Stéphanie sometimes works from home, combining colors and motifs to design next year's Christmas in the capital.

VALÉRIE

Slim, perfectly groomed and impeccably dressed, Valérie is the essence of French chic, whether she's working in her Parisian store or relaxing at her holiday home in Cap Ferret on the Atlantic coast.

We first met when friends invited us to Cap Ferret for a weekend. Valérie was at a dinner, we got talking, and conversation was easy. We discovered we had a great deal in common: we both ride horses, we both like to paint, and we both have four children. By the end of the evening we decided to meet for coffee the next day to continue our chat.

While she lives and works in Paris, Valérie loves to get out to the countryside or to the sea. She and her husband Olivier have a country house near Fontainebleau, just an hour south of Paris, where during the weekends she rides in the forest or picks up her brushes and paints.

For longer breaks, time is often spent at the family holiday home in Cap Ferret. This small peninsula of land lying west of Bordeaux is known for its beautiful properties and comfortable lifestyle. Some would say it is the Hamptons of France. Here, the rush of Paris is forgotten and Valérie's smart Parisian outfits are swapped for a casual chic wardrobe of sandals, linen shirts and pants.

There is an otherworldly feeling to this place, as if the clocks have been stopped and the trials of ordinary life are left behind. Leisurely days are savored with family and friends, eating is all about seafoods bought fresh from the fishing boats, and days are spent swimming and surfing or browsing antique stores.

Valérie's house is known for its stylish interior design and for the great dinner parties that she throws on warm summer evenings. Children, weekend guests, friends: her table hosts a mix of generations and conversation is lively. This is typical entertainment at the Cap, where dinners often start with an *aperitif* on the water's edge, and end up with guests dancing into the small hours of the next day. It doesn't matter if you're eight years old or eighty-eight; Cap Ferret is about having fun.

Back in the heart of Paris, on the beautiful Ile de la Cité, Valerie's working life is in sharp contrast to the relaxed living on the Atlantic Coast.

Several years ago Valérie and Olivier bought Maison Bosc, purveyor of gowns to the judges and lawyers of Paris since 1858. Until that time, Valérie had run a modeling agency, and had handled celebrity accounts for some of the most prestigious Parisian design houses, but she had no knowledge of the legal world, with its hierarchy and codes of order. Undaunted, the couple eagerly began building up their new business.

Valérie's first priority with Maison Bosc was to restore some of the brand's lost history. The former owner had stripped the inside of the store and a detective chase ensued as Valérie hunted down anything to do with the history of Bosc — old bills of purchase, labels, hat boxes. Today, the shop is filled to the brim with long black or red judges' robes, some trimmed in fur, some lined with silk. The details are all significant: outward signs of hierarchy.

At Cap Ferret, there is a tradition for wood cladding on the sea-front houses. As the houses age, the wood mellows and contrasts with the painted shutters and details.

The traditional fishermen's houses are built very close to each other, and their brightly colored walls are made even more cheerful by the hollyhocks that sow themselves each year along the narrow paths.

Around Valérie's main house
are smaller wooden cabins
that provide space for guests.

Visitors step over the porch and into the entrance hall to the main house. Here the white-painted wood and simple pieces of furniture set the tone.

Indoors, the dominant colors are a soft red, natural wood and a few touches of black. In summer, the long table is set outside to welcome friends to dinner.

The little boutique is two minutes' walk from the impressive Palais de Justice, and it isn't unusual for a lawyer to stop by on his way to plead in court. "Bonjour Madame, I have lost the button on my robe." Valérie smiles, "Bonjour Maitre," ("master" is how a lawyer is addressed in France). "If you don't mind waiting two minutes, we will be happy to fix that for you." Sure enough, two minutes later, a seamstress has replaced the lost button and the robe is beautifully folded and returned to the owner.

This level of service is only possible because Valérie runs the last boutique in the city to create couture robes in their own atelier adjacent to the store.

In the beginning Valérie worried about finding herself in contact with some of the most important legal minds of France. But one day, while adjusting a judge's robe, she asked if the length suited him. The reply came, "But Madame, you are the expert here!"

With this vote of confidence, Valérie started to innovate and to offer her clients new ideas. For men she created a line of silver cufflinks in motifs such as judges' caps or gavels For the women she designed linings for their gowns using couture silk scarves. These little details make all the difference.

Her role at the head of this prestigious company suits Valérie completely. She is full of an old world elegance that sets the tone for her store. She makes her clients feel privileged and respected. She is a perfectionist and lays great importance on impeccable manners and on the rules and etiquette that are an integral part of French life.

As our friendship has developed over the years since our first meeting, I never fail to enjoy a lunch or dinner in her company and the insight she provides into a privileged side to life in the capital.

YSABEL

Ysabel lives her life as she paints her canvases — carefully, thoughtfully, and in great detail. Everything around her is a source for inspiration. To step into her beautiful home in the Perche is to walk into a living painting. There is not an object, not a color in the house, nor a plant or tree in the garden that has not been given due reflection.

The beauty of this creativity is that it gives Ysabel the most pleasure when it is shared. If you stop by one morning and she says, "Stay for lunch, we'll just a have a salad," do not be fooled. This is not two slices of a tomato thrown into a bowl with a handful of lettuce. First she'll serve you coffee, then she'll take a basket and invite you to walk around the garden with her, gathering ingredients for the salad.

The informal *potager* is at the farthest side of the garden, with a nice straight path leading to it. For Ysabel, though, that direction would be way too simple: "If we go that way, I can't show you the rose I bought last spring." And so you are taken on a tour of the garden, where she shares her thoughts on rambling roses, on the perfume of irises and how to control an over enthusiastic buddleia, until finally you reach the *potager*.

An hour later, if you are lucky, the simple basket is overflowing with beautiful leaves and maybe some flowers, herbs and a few tomatoes, as well as a few wild strawberries. "Don't you love the flavor of wild strawberry in a salad dressing?" Ysabel will ask. Before you can answer comes her mused reply, "Mmm . . . I thought you would."

Back to the kitchen and she will assemble her salad with care, but with no urgency. And all the time you will be perched on a stool, enjoying every minute, watching the meal come together in the same way that you may watch an artist put the final touches to a great masterpiece.

Ysabel says that it is impossible for an artist not to like food, for its colors and flavors and the way it makes everyday objects become inspiring in their own right.

Lunch will be served on a long table that she and her husband, Jean Pierre, bought by mistake. They were so caught up in the beauty of the table and its perfect patina that they failed to notice how narrow it was, making it impossible to lay plates facing each other on opposite sides. Today they actually love its size because of the way it forces them to lay the table, staggering the settings so there is enough room for plates on the plateau and for knees below.

The meal, which was supposed to be a simple salad, is an eruption of flavors, a sensual experience that leaves you wondering why all meals can't be that way.

That is how Ysabel lives: each moment is to be savored, enjoyed, and made the most of. And that is why Ysabel and Jean Pierre bought their house.

211

The narrow table was originally a store counter. It may not make for the most practical tablescapes, but Ysabel loves the way the shape of the table echoes that of the room, and how it brings guests close together.

The color palette throughout the house is mellow, from the original *tomette* floor tiles, to the wooden fireplace surround, to the muted colors on the walls. The overall effect is one of comfort.

Ysabel and Jean Pierre spent many
hours sourcing the right furniture
to fit with the house's original
architectural details, such as the
narrow spiral staircase with its
hand-carved balustrade.

When they first saw the house, a 17th-century presbytery, it was completely overgrown — no, actually, that is an understatement; it was so overgrown that it was hard to get inside. It had stood empty for thirty years. Part of the roof was missing, the façade was invisible behind a barrier of ivy and miscellaneous self- seeded trees, and inside, water ran down the walls. They came with an estate agent to have a quick look but stayed for four hours, exploring, dreaming, and coming to terms with the idea of so much beauty just waiting to be reawakened.

The presbytery stands beside the church in the center of the village and had housed the local priest. In the time since Ysabel and Jean Pierre moved in, little by little the village has been re-inhabited and transformed from a sleepy and nearly empty cluster of houses to a chocolate-box village, where any passing traffic inevitably slows down just to admire the beauty of the place.

Before living here Ysabel and Jean Pierre lived in Paris. Both are artists and admit that they longed to get out of Paris because they were tired of the stress of city life. They hoped to find some tranquility in the country, a place with plenty of space for them both to create.

There was nothing reasonable in their purchase of the presbytery. They knew it would be costly to restore, but once they had seen it there was no going back. This is the place they had to live. It had chosen them before they chose it — some moves have more to do with destiny than with pragmatic decisions.

And so the restoration work began. For six months they drove out from Paris every week to supervise the main work that was going on in their absence. But, as soon as they had water and electricity, although still no heating, they fled the capital and moved in for good.

The first winter was very, very cold. During the next two years they completed the major work and decorated their new home beautifully. Of course, Ysabel will tell you that there is still a lot to do, but one must acknowledge that a house of this age is an ongoing project, a work of art that continues to live and be lived in.

Part of the first floor has been made into a charming guest room and bathroom, with a breathtaking view over the garden on one side and onto the church on the other. Ysabel welcomes bed and breakfast guests here, and when I was lucky enough to stay there I sat for a while in the morning simply enjoying the extraordinary view from the open window and the feeling of being pampered.

Ysabel has a real passion for her garden. She created a layout that complements the façade of the house and that leads the visitor from one flower bed to the next. There are tables and chairs dotted here and there, to be favored according to the season and to where the light falls.

The soil is rich and fertile and the roses are happy. She works with colors that pair well with the soft beige stone and the grey

shutters of the façade. As a result, she has created a harmonious space that looks good in any light and in any season.

As if decorating the house, tending her garden, and welcoming guests to her B&B aren't enough, Ysabel is also a successful and prolific painter. She trained as an artist at the Penningen School in Paris, one of the most renowned art schools in the capital. Her paintings often portray everyday objects — a bowl caught in a certain light, a pair of shoes, a spoon. Her palette is full of the greys and blues that color her memories of childhood days along the shoreline of St. Malo.

Jean Pierre is a sculptor and together they hold an open house to show their work each year. To begin with, this was limited to close friends, but it has slowly grown. Their last edition saw over 200 people walk through the door of their home.

Their growing popularity risks becoming invasive, and they tell me that the time has come to rethink their shows and come back to the essentials: their pleasure in creating and their delight in the small, everyday qualities of life — walking the dog, catching the last light of a summer's day in the garden, and working quietly in their studios.

Here in their country home, their haven of peace, they both understand that inspiration is vital to creation and that it is best sought in the quiet enjoyment of everyday pleasures.

Ysabel has divided the modest-sized garden into an interesting flow of outdoor rooms.

Inspiration to paint is everywhere, be it a flower in the garden or a collection of antique brushes.

Tall windows bathe the painting studio in natural light, allowing Ysabel to set up her easels and work comfortably on her canvases.

THE GIRLFRIENDS' RECOMMENDATIONS

Alicia

Her Warehouse: on appointment only
+33 (0)6 11 82 06 94
folavrile@hotmail.fr

Cheese: "Charlotte Milhiet"
Ferme du bois normand, Rueil la Gadelière

Bakery: "La boulangerie Motrot"
la Ferté vidame

Catherine

Her Hotel: Chateau de la Marine
18 rue Rupembert, 62126 Wimille
+33 (0)3 21 99 80 33
www.chateaudelamarine.com

Winery: la Vigne au verre
1 rue Jean Marie Bourguignon 62930 Wimereux
+33 (0)3 21 32 92 38

Florist: l'Agave
99 rue Carnot 62930 Wimereux
+33 (0)3 21 83 75 46

Fish Market: Quai Gambetta à Boulogne sur
 mer

Cécile

Her Store: Chez Nous Campagne
Le Relais du bourg, 28340 Rohaire
+33 (0)2 37 37 67 88
www.chez-nous-campagne.com

Farm-Food-Shop: David Simoen
Ferme de l'Etoile, l'Hôtel Neveu, 61400
 Courgeon
+33 (0)2 33 25 10 67

Decoration: Le Bazar des fees
12 rue notre Dame, 61400 Mortagne au Perche
+33 (0)2 33 85 59 09

Celestina

Her Wedding Gowns: Celestina Agostino
15, rue de l'abbé grégoire, Paris
+33 (0)1 45 44 76 14
celestina-agostino.com

Couture Clothes: Gisele So
50 rue de Sèvres Paris 75007
+33 (0)1 46 03 37 79
www.giseleso.fr

Hotel: le Plaza Athenée
25 ave Montaigne, Paris 75008
+33 (0)1 53 67 66 65

Hairdresser: Carita Montaigne
3 rue bocadour, 75008 Paris
www.maisondebeautecarita.fr

Charlotte

Food: Hotel Baudy
81 rue Claude Monet, 27620 Giverny
+33 (0)2 32 21 10 03
www.restaurantbaudy.com

Decoration: Caravanne
6, rue Pavée - 75004 Paris
+33 (0)1 44 61 04 20
www.caravane.fr/en

Christelle

Her Store: Bord de Scène
23 rue de la Messe, Villez sous Bailleul, 27950
+33 (0)2 32 52 46 18
instagram.com/borddescene

Food: street market in Pacy sur Eure

Hotel: L'épicerie du Pape
5 Rue de la Ferme, 27910 Vascœuil
+33 (0)2 35 23 64 37

Brocante: Brocante de la Bruyere
32 rue campion, 60880 Le Meux
www.brocantedelabruyere.com

Claire

Her art: Gibbs Smith
Chateau de Beauvoir, 03330 Echassieres
+33 (0)6 07 84 79 27
www.clairebasler.com

Florist: Pierre Kavaciuk
Paris
+33 (0)6 74 43 82 50

Paint: Maison Marin
70 avenue Gabriel Péri, 94111 Arceuil
+33 (0)1 47 40 92 59

Clarisse

Her Flower Shop: Atelier Vertumne
12 rue de la Sourdiere, Paris 75001
+33 (0)1 42 86 06 76
www.atelier-vertumne.fr

Restaurant: Crudus
21 rue Saint Roch
+33 (0)1 42 60 90 29

Hairdresser: Alain Bernard
38 rue de la Sourdiere, Paris 75001
+33 (0)1 42 60 61 50

Herborist: l'Herboristerie du Palais Royal
11 rue des petits champs, Paris 75001
+33 (0)1 42 97 54 68
www.herboristerie.com/

Cornélie

Restaurant: Ma Cocotte
106 Rue des Rosiers, 93400 Saint-Ouen
+33 (0)1 49 51 70 00

Café: La Favorite
39 Rue de Passy, 75016
+33 (0)1 42 88 20 53

Clothing: Tara Jarmon
51 rue de passy 75016
+33 (0)1 45 24 65 20

Evelyne

Her Champagne: Champagne Boizel
46 avenue de champagne
+33 (0)3 26 55 21 51
www.boizel.com

Café: le café du Palais
14 place Myron Herrick 51100 Reims.
+33 (0)3 26 47 52 54
www.cafedupalais.fr

222

Bakery: Biscuits Fossier
25 cours Jean-Baptiste Langlet, 51100 Reims
www.fossier.fr

Frédérique

Her Château: Chateau d'Emalleville
17, rue de l'Église, 27930 Emalleville
+33 (0)2 32 34 01 87
www.chateaudemalleville.com

Restaurant: La Ferme de Haute Cremonville
27430 Saint-Étienne-du-Vauvray
+33 (0)2 32 59 14 22
www.restaurant-ferme-haute-cremonville.com

Shoes: Freelance
65 Rue Saint-Nicolas, 76000 Rouen
+33 (0)2 35 70 08 00
www.freelance.fr

Horse Riding Equipment: Padd
Long Buisson 27930 Guichainville
+33 (0)2 32 36 95 07

Laure

Her Designs: Maison Caumont
+33 (0)1 82 09 89 33
www.maisoncaumont.com

Restaurant: Luisa Maria
12 Rue Monsieur le Prince, 75006 Paris
+33(0)1 43 29 62 49

Decoration: Les Fleurs
6 Passage Josset, 75011 Paris
01 43 55 12 94

Books: Le Marché aux livres
parc George Brassens 75015, Paris

Marie

Her Sculptures: Marie Christophe
+33 (0)6 03 22 77 48
www.mariechristophe.com

Chocolates: Jean Paul Hevin
41 rue de Bretagne, 75003 Paris
+33 (0)1 44 61 94 43
www.jeanpaulhevin.com/en

Shoes: Roger Vivier
29 rue du Faubourg St Honoré, 75008 Paris
+33 (0)1 53 43 00 85
www.rogervivier.com

Beauty Products: Buly
6 rue Bonaparte, 75006 Paris
+33 (0)1 43 29 02 50
www.buly1803.com/en

Marie-Christine

Her Château: Chateau de Moissac
Moissac Bellevue 83630
+33 (0)6 07 39 37 09
www.chateaudemoissac.fr

Fine Food: L'Epicerie
7 rue Marechal Foch. 83630 Aups
+33 (0)4 94 84 03 11

Olive Oil: Chateau de Taurenne
5800 rte de Tourtour. 83630 Aups
+33 (0)4 98 10 21 35
www.domaine-de-taurenne.fr

Pottery: Ferme de la Celestine
chemin du plan.83630 Moissac bellevue
+33 (0)4 94 60 16 52

Nathalie

Her Garden: Les Jardins du Mirail
Le Mirail, 72540 Crannes en Champagne
+33 (0)2 43 88 05 50

Clothing: Amin Kader
2 rue Guisarde 75006 Paris

Paints: Sennelier
3 quai Voltaire 75007 Paris
+33(0)1 42 60 72 15

Sabine

Her Gallery: Galerie Sabine Puget
Château Barras, 83670 Fox-Amphoux
33(0)6 16 01 54 58
www.galeriesabinepuget.com

Restaurant: Chez Jean et Chantal
83670 Fox-Amphoux
+33(0)4 94 80 70 76

Food: Gare du Nord
10a rue Maréchal Foch,83630 Aups
+33(0)6 41 67 21 89 Website

Florist: l'Armalette
chemin de la piscine, Sillans la Cascade
+33(0)4 94 04 67 83
www.pepiniere-armalette.fr

Sophie

Her Painted Porcelain: Sophie Masson
www.sophiemasson.com

Goat's Cheese: Chevrerie Sorene
48800 Les Aydons
www.chevrerie-sorene.fr

Pottery: La boutique Appart
rue droite, 07140 les Vans

Ceramics Museum: Sèvres - Cité de la céramique
2 Place de la Manufacture, 92310 Sèvres
+33(0)1 46 29 22 00
www.sevresciteceramique.fr

Stéphanie

Her Design Agency: 2 Win Display
www.2windisplay.com

Restaurant: Le Café aux Ministères
9 avenue de Saxe 75007 Paris

Street Market: Marché de Saxe-Breteuil
avenue de Saxe 75007 Paris

Theatre: Théâtre des Champs-Élysées
15 Avenue Montaigne, 75008 Paris
+33 (0)1 49 52 50 00

Valérie

Her Store: La Maison Bosc
3 boulevard du Palais, 75004 Paris
+33 (0)1 43 54 16 50
www.maisonbosc.com

Restaurant: Chez Hortense
Avenue du sémaphore, Lège Cap Ferret, 33970
+33 (0)5 56 60 62 56
www.chez-hortense.fr

Hotel: Maison du Bassin
5 rue des Pionniers - 33950 Lège Cap-Ferret
+33 (0)5 56 60 60 63
www.lamaisondubassin.com

Antiques: Esprit du Cap
2 rue des pionniers, 33950 Cap Ferret
+33 (0)5 56 60 67 79
www.espritducap.com

Ysabel

Her Hotel: Le Presbytère de Préaux-du-Perche
+33 (0)2 33 73 58 91
www.entre-voir.com

Chocolates: Charles Bataille
14 boulevard Bansard des Bois 61130 Bellême
+33 (0)2 33 73 41 02

Tea Salon: Le Comptoir du Porche
Rue Ville Close 61130 Bellême
+33 (0)2 33 73 15 00

Florist: Gabrielle Feuillard
1, place au Blé, 61130 Bellême
+33 (0)2 33 73 00 94

UN GRAND MERCI

There is no doubt that writing a book is a team effort, I don't think I realized just how true that is until I started working on this project. I would have been totally lost were it not for the support and encouragement of many exceptional people.

First of all, I thank my stylish girlfriends, who opened their doors with such generosity.

Thank you to my children, Victor, Ella, Nina and Jim, for their unending support and enthusiasm and, of course, *merci* to my husband, Eric, for his well-chosen words of advice and encouragement.

I was fortunate to work with Franck Schmitt; his talent as a photographer and his ability to make me laugh made our photo shoots such fun.

I am grateful to Madge Baird, my editor, for inviting me to write and for holding my hand every step of the way, and to the design team, Sheryl Dickert and Renee Bond, for their skill and their patience with my many requests.

And, finally, to those special friends who I could call on at every stage of the book for an honest opinion, a word of advice or a timely suggestion — Tish, Yorn, Yves, Rita, and Betty Lou — thank you. You know how precious your help has been.

224

Sharon Santoni grew up in England but married a Frenchman and has raised her family in Normandy, France. Her blog, *My French Country Home,* is read daily by thousands all over the world. She writes about daily life in rural France; the ups and downs of family life; her inspiring French girlfriends; the intricacies of village life; and her love of searching for brocante treasure in the flea markets of Paris and the countryside.